For my children, Kristina, Courtney, and Elena.
My greatest hope is that this book will help you
grow into maturity.

—Richard Raben

For Sri Chinmoy,
poet, artist, athlete, musician, goodwill
ambassador, and beloved spiritual mentor,
who amazingly lives every second
boldly, lovingly, and completely.
Your example allowed me to know that
heroism *is* possible, and inspired any
wisdom that I've included in this book.

—Hiyaguha Cohen

CONTENTS

ACKNOWLEDGMENTS

This book is the culmination of a twenty-nine-year interest in *Star Trek* and its applications to everyday life in the twentieth century. I thank Gene Roddenberry for his vision and presentation of the *Star Trek* universe.

I thank my three daughters, Kristina, Courtney, and Elena, for their love. They are the reason for this book. My motivation for writing this book was to help children and adults all over the world realize their potential.

I thank my collaborator, Hiyaguha Cohen, and her husband, Sudheya Rosenberg, for helping me bring these ideas to life. Even though we have had our ups and downs, I respect and appreciate Hiyaguha's writing talent and her commitment to this project.

I thank Sandra Choron, our literary agent, for her expertise and her friendship. Her enthusiasm and hard work are greatly responsible for the publication of this book.

I thank our editors, Liza Dawson at William Morrow and Stephen Power at Avon Books. They have worked tirelessly to improve our manuscript. I also thank Ron Schaumburg for his editorial assistance on short notice.

I thank Leslie Brody, Ph.D., for his coaching in the early stages of this project. His enthusiasm and creativity helped me to continue through difficult times. I thank Marla Spellenberg for her support and graphics assistance. She is a committed *Star Trek* fan and has been a sounding board for my ideas. I thank Daena Giardella, a wonderful actress and teacher, for her help with some of the exercises in this book. I thank Jack Murphy for helping me understand how some of my original ideas could be presented in book form. I thank my good friends Bob Babikian and Aaron White for their support, friendship, encouragement, and love during a very difficult period in my life. I thank my sister, Carol Alexander, for always being there for me. Her kindness, loyalty, and compassion have been an inspiration to me.

And lastly, I want to thank *Star Trek* fans everywhere for sharing my love of the *Star Trek* universe.

—Richard Raben

※

First, foremost, and with all my heart, I thank my husband, Sudheya Rosenberg—a brilliant editor and committed *Star Trek* fan—who read and critiqued every word I wrote. He contributed so many ideas and editorial suggestions that his name really belongs on the cover.

Next there's Richard Raben, who came up with the wonderful idea that gave birth to this book, providing me with an excuse to watch endless hours of *Star Trek* reruns while indulging in my favorite activities—writing and thinking about inspiring things.

I feel extremely lucky to have had Liza Dawson at William Morrow and Stephen Power at Avon Books for editors. Liza not only offered vision, expertise, and great ideas, but also support and kindness when the pressure was on. And Stephen steered the project from beginning to end with the skill of a Starfleet captain—with his vast *Trek* knowledge, accessibility, and attention to detail.

I'm enthusiastically seconding Rich's thanks to Sandra Choron, our agent, who believed wholeheartedly in this book from the very beginning and who went beyond the normal agenting duties to cheerlead and keep us sane, even at a time when she suffered great personal loss. And also to Ron Schaumburg, for pitching in and accomplishing an amazing amount in a very short, frenzied time.

I also want to thank the many people who offered friendship and support and who helped me survive the crazy writing schedule this book demanded. Suchesta Flynn and Susanne Wissell in particular, for checking in constantly, volunteering to help with everything from massages to domestic chores, and for putting up with the fact that I've had little time to socialize over the past months. Also Chalanta O'Connell for his happy willingness to draw on his endless knowledge of history and trivia to find some of the real-life examples that appear in the book. Same for my mom, Fay Cohen, who had some sterling suggestions. Then there's Vanda Sendzimer and other writing friends who offered so much encouragement. And finally, the staff at the Mass Resource Center in Ayer, Massachusetts, who let me use their space and equipment and even acted as guinea pigs for the Self-Assessment Test. Oops — almost forgot Temptations, also in Ayer, a wonderful coffee café where I sat for many hours writing, dreaming, and fueling up on delicious confections and java creations.

Much of the inspiration for what I've written comes from the few extraordinarily heroic souls who I've been blessed enough to know in my life, especially Ida Rosenberg, my grandmother-in-law. Her overflowing love for life, radiant joy, and unfailing ability to see (and evoke) the best in everybody transformed all who met her, including me, though I knew her far too briefly. I thought of her often while writing this book.

And finally, like Richard, I want to thank Gene Roddenberry and everyone who shares a love of *Star Trek*. I thought I'd get sick of *Star Trek* watching so many episodes back-to-back and immersing myself in the various shows day and night. Instead, I've grown to love *Star Trek* more than ever and to appreciate even more just how wise, visionary, and compassionate the *Star Trek* universe is.

—Hiyaguha Cohen

INTRODUCTION

If you watch Star Trek, *look for yourself. You will be there.*
— Yvonne Fern, *Gene Roddenberry: The Last Conversation*

In the 1960s, college student Richard Raben was depressed. He had little hope for his future. He thought the world was a disaster. He wondered what he was living for. If it wasn't for *Star Trek*, he might have become a bum.

Star Trek gave Richard a weekly reprieve from his bleak existence. It let him experience a world where people didn't act like jerks and the brighter side of human nature always prevailed. Eventually, Richard flunked out of his pre-med program and dashed his mother's dreams of having a doctor for a son. Guilty and teetering on the brink of despair, he turned to the *Enterprise* for solace. There, he saw Kirk face disasters even more dreadful than his. Kirk's courage and sense of mission inspired him, and he soon found himself conjuring up Kirk at will, using Kirk's example to get through his own dilemmas. It didn't take long to figure out that he could look to Spock for help in making tough decisions, and to Scotty to convince himself that *nothing* is impossible.

Eventually, Richard discovered his niche, pursuing studies in Jungian psychology and dramatic storytelling. Now armed with a theoretical framework, he reflected on how his *Star Trek* heroes had pulled him through adolescent anomie, and realized that *Star Trek* provides a modern-day source of heroic archetypes in a world woefully devoid of heroes. These archetypes are just as powerful and affecting as the ancient mythical characters that influenced Jung's theories.

Flash forward: 1995. Richard met Hiyaguha Cohen, a writer who had deep experience in clinical counseling and metaphysics—and who was a *Star Trek* aficionado herself. She immediately grasped the significance of the ideas that Raben had been germinating and saw how they could be applied to help people improve their day-to-day lives. Together, Raben and Cohen decided to go where no writer had gone before: helping people tap the heroic potential within themselves by identifying with the qualities of the *Star Trek* heroes whom they love so much.

And people do love the *Star Trek* heroes. In America alone, 53 percent of all people consider themselves *Star Trek* fans. Like Richard Raben, the fans of *Star Trek* love the show because it explores not only outer space, but also the inner reaches of the human psyche. In the very last episode of *The Next Generation*, Q tells Picard, "This is the exploration that awaits you: Not mapping stars and studying nebulae, but charting the unknown possibilities of existence." This books begins where *The Next Generation* leaves off.

Boldly Live As You've Never Lived Before leads you on an unprecedented inner voyage, where you'll discover new worlds of possibility inside of your own being. Unlike other self-help books, this one doesn't merely explore what makes you tick; it also reveals what you can become. You are a hero in the making—a hero like Kirk, Picard, Sisko, Janeway, and the various other *Star Trek* crewmembers. Right now, you may not feel terribly heroic, but as you read on, you'll discover that you actually have a lot in common with your favorite *Star Trek* heroes. You'll also learn that the *Star Trek* characters can help you to become ever more heroic; in fact, you can employ them as personal guides in your journey of self-transformation.

In each of the *Star Trek* series, you find four types of heroes: **Warriors,** like Worf, Kira, Scotty, and B'Elanna; **Analysts,** like Spock, Data, Odo, and Tuvok; **Relaters,** like Guinan, McCoy, Troi, and Kes; and **Leaders,** like Kirk, Picard, Sisko, and Janeway. Each type of hero has a unique constellation of strengths and can inspire you in a distinct way. If you have lots of fears and let people push you around, you might need a little kick in the pants from a fearless Warrior like Worf. If you have trouble making big decisions or taking responsibility, you need to spend time absorbing the focused energy of a Leader like Kirk or Picard. If your love life is going nowhere, perhaps you should call on the compassion and empathy of Relaters like Troi, Kes, or McCoy. Or it may be that your feelings are in such turmoil that a dose of logic and reasoning from Analysts like Spock or Data will set you back on course. This book will help you to draw on the strengths of the various *Star Trek* characters to help you navigate through life's challenges.

But living boldly doesn't merely mean taking help from great mentors. It also means becoming a great hero yourself. As this book will show, you already have heroic qualities inside of you in abundance, but right now you don't manifest them very often because fear and self-doubt and laziness and other problems stand in your way. You'll find hands-on exercises in the chapters that follow to help you consciously invoke your innate heroic nature and bring it forward in your everyday life.

The first thing you'll do is discover *your* predominant heroic type. As you read on, you'll make an inventory of your likenesses to each character so you can determine if you're a Warrior, Leader, Relater, or Analyst. You'll also find out which character types you don't resemble at all and most need to learn from. Learning about your type will help you make sense of things in your life, like why you always fall in love with the same type of people; why you always end up in jobs that pay dog wages; why you can't give up any cause you undertake, even when it's obviously hopeless.

You'll also start to notice that among your friends, relatives, and colleagues there are aggressive go-getters (Warriors), impossible romantics (Relaters), visionaries (Leaders), and realists (Analysts). Of course, you don't want to categorize people out-of-hand, but knowing a person's type can help you show more compassion and tolerance for that individual. You'll finally understand, for instance, that your boss can't tolerate errors not because he has it in for you, but because he has the Analyst's drive for perfection; or that your spouse cries at every silly romantic movie she sees not because she's unhinged, but because she has the Relater's extraordinary sensitivity. Knowing these things about people lets you communicate with them in a language they can understand.

Of course, every personality type has its gems—and its losers. In the same way that few apple pies come close to Mom's home-baked—even though every pie has both apples and crust—few Warriors have Worf's courage or honor, although all have his aggressive edge. Few leaders have Picard's integrity or ability to inspire, although all know how to command, and so on. To become a true hero, you need to bring forward the sublime aspects of your predominant type and to drop the not-so-inspiring aspects. You also need a good mix of heroic qualities. If you have all Leader qualities and no Relater traits, you'll be unbearably bossy. If you relate well to everybody but have no Warrior, you'll get trampled on and used by people. And so, your job is to develop a smorgasbord of heroic traits. The Self-Assessment Test in Chapter 3 will clearly indicate where you need work, which heroic qualities you most need to develop.

So read on. This book will help you change from an occasional, closet hero to a full-fledged Starfleet-ready champion. All you need to do is take some lessons from the Starfleet crews, and then put into practice what you learn. You'll definitely succeed, not only because you'll have learned from the best teachers in the universe, but also because you already have all the ingredients of heroism within you. As the mystic poet Sri Chinmoy says, "You have a strong hope, you have a firm faith, you have a stark arrow in hand. . . . Who else can be the changer of world history?"

PART ONE

IT TAKES MORE THAN WARP

DRIVE TO GET RESPECT

1

NOBILITY, COURAGE, AND ABSOLUTELY

NO CELLULITE: HEROES IN SPACE

[Heroism] is about leaping off the edge of the known to confront the unknown, and trusting that when the time comes, we will have what we need to face our dragons, discover our treasures, and return to transform our kingdom.
— Carol Pearson, *Awakening the Hero Within*

Christopher Columbus . . . Francisco Pizarro . . . Ferdina Magellan . . . These intrepid souls all ventured forth in the unknown, pitted their puny resources against the ele ments, and explored strange new worlds. Sounds like a typi mission aboard the Starship *Enterprise*, doesn't it?

Except that whenever these heroes landed in a new place, th had little patience for the bothersome natives who got in their way. Cranky from their long journeys, eager to start plundering, they enslaved the local residents—or annihilated them.

How different the planet would be today if the South Pacific had been visited not by James Cook but by James Kirk, if the coast of Florida had been discovered not by Ponce de León but by Jean-Luc Picard, or if Western Europe and Britain had been visited not by Julius Caesar but by Kathryn Janeway!

In their journeys throughout the universe, the *Star Trek* crews often encounter alien beings. Does Kirk ever attempt to enslave the strange creatures he meets? Does Picard charge into battle against them? Hardly! Our *Star Trek* heroes invariably find a way to communicate with the aliens, turning fear and hostility into understanding and goodwill.

Look at what happens in the Classic *Star Trek* episode "The Devil in the Dark," when Horta, a bizarre-looking silicon-based life form, kills the human miners who penetrate her underground territory. The humans fear and loathe her, and understandably want to protect themselves against her—so they set out to destroy her. But when Kirk encounters Horta, he senses that she is an intelligent creature, and can't bring himself to kill her. Spock also senses intelligence in Horta, so he reaches out his hand and mind-melds with her, risking his life. He discovers that Horta has no evil intent; instead, she is a mother who kills humans only because she wants to protect her nest of silicon eggs, which the humans have been harvesting. In the end, Horta and the humans reach understanding and avert war. What's more, the miners establish profitable trade relations with her. Kirk could have destroyed Horta easily. But instead of moving in with phasers firing, he communicated with her, respecting her as a fellow living being.

Not that Kirk and his Starfleet compatriots are wimps. Far from it. When they have no other choice, they rage into battle with steadfast determination, always outmaneuvering their opponents. You won't find better warriors than Kirk and company anywhere in the galaxy. But unlike so many real-life heroes from our history, the *Star Trek* characters offer much more than swashbuckling courage and a willingness to sacrifice their lives for some cause. Yes, they are brave and quick—but they also are creative, optimistic, poised, compassionate, wise, kind, tolerant, funny, and totally disinterested in personal gain. Where else in our hero-starved lives do we find such inspiring people?

Certainly not in the headlines. The media constantly bombards us with stories about our once-heroes now in hot water for doing something unthinkable. Woody Allen turns out to be a cradle robber. Mike Tyson beat up his wife. Nixon spied on his opponents. Prince Charles cheated on Di. Kurt Waldheim cooperated with the Nazis. The parade of dethroned greats goes on and on, leaving the planet nearly bereft of role models.

No wonder we look to the skies for signs of hope! No wonder we look to *Star Trek* for heroes! Would Spock use his powers of logic to find innovative ways to cheat on his income tax? Certainly not. Would Picard promote a land scam? Inconceivable. Starfleet officers don't do ignoble things. On the contrary, in episode after episode, the *Star Trek* crewmembers risk life and limb to help others. If another ship needs help, the *Enterprise* rushes to the rescue, no matter how great the danger. If a risky mission must be carried out, everybody aboard volunteers. How often in real life do we observe such nonchalant willingness to die for altruistic reasons?

Certainly not too often, but remarkably, brave souls *do* show up on Earth now and again. For instance, Joan of Arc—inspired by voices from heaven—led the French Army into battle when she was merely sixteen years old. One hundred and fifty years later, Sir Thomas More, the English statesman and adviser to King Henry VIII, stood by his Catholic beliefs and opposed his boss's decision to divorce his wife—at risk of death. And in our own century, Mohandas Gandhi endured years of imprisonment and numerous life-threatening fasts in his campaign to win Indian independence from the British. Each of these heroes paid the ultimate price. Joan, denounced as a heretic, was turned into French toast when she was burned at the stake. By sticking his neck out, More got his head chopped off. And Gandhi was assassinated by a religious fanatic.

The message of *Star Trek* is that such heroism is the province not only of a few extraordinary souls, now dead, but of every human being on earth. Gene Roddenberry, the creator of the *Star Trek* series, said: "*Star Trek*'s message is really to increase capacity, to become more open and less fearful . . . *to become all that we are capable of becoming."* If you *ever* found the capacity within yourself to "rise above yourself"—even for a fleeting instant—then you have the capacity to do so again and again. If one person on earth ever acted heroically, then surely the rest of us can do so. After all, we all have the same basic biochemistry, impulses, and needs. Repetition is the law of nature.

You may be thinking, "Who, me? I'm no hero. I just get a vicarious thrill watching someone else boldly go where I've never gone." *But there is a hero within you.* That's why you respond to *Star Trek* the way that you do. Think of it this way: If you don't understand Greek, you can't appreciate a play by Sophocles performed in the original language. If you've never tasted ice cream, you won't salivate when you see a hot fudge sundae. You wouldn't respond to the *Star Trek* heroes the way you do unless you already had a hero somewhere inside yourself.

Gene Roddenberry certainly believed that all of us have heroes within us. He once remarked, "I have found in so many, many people evidence of heroism, the ability to perform heroic acts." And again, in an interview shortly before his death, he said, "Our heroes help define us, help us choose the attributes we wish to have, the qualities that may very well be within us, are within us, or we wouldn't pick those particular people for heroes."

Everywhere we look we see evidence of ordinary people doing extraordinary things: volunteers who work tirelessly to rescue victims from buildings destroyed by earthquakes or terrorist bombs; doctors who rush to regions devastated by plagues; people who overcome physical handicaps to complete marathons; workers who quit lucrative jobs to begin entirely new careers at midlife. Unfortunately, stories about such everyday heroics rarely make big news, getting lost in the avalanche of sensationalistic tales that dominate the media. And so, we lose sight of the fact that heroes surround us, and that we may occasionally even act as heroes ourselves.

In fact, there have probably been dozens of incidents in your own life when you've acted heroically. Maybe you treated someone with kindness in spite of your impulse to act hatefully. Or you ran a marathon, or worked long hours to put yourself through school, or spoke the truth even though it put you in danger or made someone angry.

Okay, so it's not the same as beaming down to the surface of a hostile planet or refusing to buckle under Cardassian torture. But heroics don't always need to be as grand as an attempt on Mt. Everest. As Robert Kennedy says in the introduction to John F. Kennedy's *Profiles in Courage*:

> Without belittling the courage with which men have died, we should not forget those acts of courage with which men have *lived*. A man does what he must—in spite of personal consequences, in spite of obstacles and dangers and pressures—and that is the basis of all human morality. To be courageous . . . requires no exceptional qualifications, no magic formula, no special combination of time, place, and circumstance.

The fact is, if you ever did *anything* heroic in your life, you can do more. The *Star Trek* crewmembers do just the sort of heroic things you've done on those rare golden moments in your past, only they do such things more often and in more dramatic ways (and they do them while millions of people are watching). Maybe you couldn't muster Jean-Luc Picard's incorruptible virtue at this particular moment; you might have trouble invoking Kirk's fear-nothing-in-the-universe courage. Even so, even if you have a long way to go before you qualify for Starfleet Academy, you *do* have the potential within you to be great and heroic: We all do. The heroic instinct is inherent in the human psyche. To excel, to be special, to make a difference—these values propel us through life, sometimes in spite of ourselves.

Unfortunately, because we don't really believe we can be heroes, we settle for the next best thing: outdoing other people—twisting and perverting our own highest impulses. We want to excel, but we're afraid of failing, so we push our kids or our spouses to succeed in our stead. We attempt to be special, not by achieving our fullest potential, but by laboring to smash the competition, by owning a flashier car or a faster computer. We want to make a difference, but we do so by trying to dominate the world rather than by living harmoniously within it.

How many kids in street gangs act out their heroic instincts—although in a distorted way—through bravado and violence? They want to take a risk, do something new, test their limits. They long to explore uncharted territory, and so they join the gang. Unfortunately, in the gang, the only way to act out heroic instincts—the only way to impress the posse—is through crime and violence. Likewise, how many ruthless business people could become true heroes if they only applied their determination and cunning to some noble cause? They outwit the IRS, demolish their competitors, gain riches and power for themselves. Using the same canny abilities, they *could* score victory for the greater good.

Do we humans persist in our negativity and self-indulgence because we're made of lesser stuff than Kirk or Sisko? No! The same impulse that drives our heroes to be great drives us to buy more, want more, push more, compete more. It's the urge to transcend, move forward—but manifested in a vastly different form. The trick is to harness that driving urge and always focus it in a positive direction.

You think that all this talk about having a hero inside doesn't apply to *you?* That you couldn't possibly become a true hero, especially considering your current state of consciousness? Well, other people have certainly made the leap from uninspired existence to full-fledged heroism—and without coming to tragic ends like Joan of Arc or Gandhi. Look to the example of people like the founders of Alcoholics Anonymous—Bill W., a stockbroker, and Bob S., a doctor—both "hopeless" alcoholics. They both realized that drinking was ruining their lives, and in an inspired moment agreed to help each other stay sober. They not only managed to confront and conquer their own problems, but developed principles and strategies that now help millions of people throughout the world. Did Bob and Bill consider themselves heroic? It's doubtful, yet like all the heroes of history, they overcame their personal demons and left a legacy to inspire others.

Abraham Lincoln provides another example. He failed in business numerous times, lost elections numerous times, even had a nervous breakdown, and yet now we consider him one of the greatest heroes in American history. An amusing story about Lincoln makes it clear that he saw himself as just an ordinary guy: Back when Lincoln was a country lawyer, a fellow came to him before a trial and offered him $100 if he would deliberately throw a case. "Absolutely not," Lincoln replied. The other guy upped the ante to $500. Again Lincoln refused. When the fellow suggested that maybe $1,000 was a more reasonable offer, Lincoln grabbed him by the shoulders and threw him down the stairs. The guy dusted himself off and said, "I guess what they say about you is true—you're an honest man." And Lincoln said, "It's not that. You're just getting too close to my price."

The list of one-time losers who eventually excelled goes on and on. Albert Einstein didn't even start talking until he was six years old! After that, his school performance was barely average. More recently, Maya Angelou had a stint as a prostitute before becoming a great writer invited to recite poetry at a presidential inauguration. People like these testify to the capacity all humans have to overcome problems and flaws and make a real difference in the world.

If you read about the lives of great people such as these, one thing you'll notice is that almost all of them had somebody special in their lives who gave them strength and faith. Maybe an extraordinarily strong grandparent, or a neighbor, or a teacher—a mentor of sorts. We too need to find somebody to help us along. Although we already have the elements of heroism within us, we need inspiration and guidance to call forth our higher nature, in the same way that a budding violinist needs to hear accomplished musicians play in order to improve. Unfortunately, the heroes of history probably won't do it for us. Though we may get inspiration from hearing about their lives, we forget what they teach us in a flash. Their lives seem remote, distant, and qualitatively different from ours. We know only a few facts about them, not how they handled the type of day-to-day challenges we must confront. So where will we find *our* mentors? In the *Star Trek* universe, of course.

Because we have access to technology, the *Star Trek* heroes can actually come alive whenever we choose to invoke their presence. At the touch of a button they appear in our homes on our TV screens. So real have these figures become, so pervasive a part of the cultural landscape, that we know more about them—their dreams, fears, strengths, life-histories—than about real-life greats. We may even know more about them than we do about our own family or friends.

Watching *Star Trek*, we see the crewmembers up close and personal. Just like us, they grapple with challenging situations every day. They suffer illness, loneliness, the death of friends. They wrestle with their own—and each other's—dislikes and quirks and incompetencies. They encounter horrible creatures as well as beings more talented than themselves, and they face the unknown, just like we do. Invariably, no matter what the situation, they meet it with courage, dignity, and integrity. And in the end, they always triumph.

It doesn't matter that the *Star Trek* characters are fictional. Throughout history, we humans have always sought guidance and inspiration from mythological figures: Hercules, a man of great strength; Odysseus, a brave seafarer of enormous cunning; King Arthur, who commanded his knights to search for the Holy Grail; White Buffalo Woman, who brought the sacred pipe to the Sioux and taught the people how to live.

Now *Star Trek* has become our modern mythology, a vivid and vibrant part of our collective consciousness as we hurtle toward the twenty-first century. Kirk, Picard, Sisko, Janeway, and their crews—these characters embody for us all the qualities of the classical mythological heroes. Bravery. Skill. Intelligence. Loyalty. Selflessness. And—whether Vulcan, Klingon, android, or Earthling—they reveal to us our own highest possibilities.

For example, in the final episode of *The Next Generation*, Picard must fly his spaceship right into the heart of a space anomaly in order to save humanity—a sure suicide mission. He has no qualms about sacrificing his own life, but his crew wavers. He turns everyone around with a speech so rousing, so inspiring, that if you could leap through the screen and join the crew, you probably would.

> All I can say is that . . . although we have been together
> for a short time, I know that you are the finest crew in the
> fleet . . . and I would trust each of you with my life.

Who can listen to Picard's great speech without feeling an inner thrill? Who can watch Kirk defeat his foes time and again, against all odds, without cheering inwardly? Or see Spock sacrifice his life to save the ship in *The Wrath of Khan* without skipping a heartbeat?

Week after week, the *Star Trek* crews wrangle not just with hostile aliens and calamities on distant planets but with psychological, moral, and spiritual problems as well. Unlike many mythological and historical heroes, Kirk and company do more than slay dragons and defeat the foe: They also confront their *inner* demons and strive to be impeccable in every possible aspect of life.

The *Star Trek* crews care deeply about the environment, about social problems, and about the future of humanity, and they act on these concerns. They treat each other with respect and kindness, valuing the differences among them; they maintain implicit faith in their own abilities; they cherish their own creativity and special interests; they like to laugh; they see the good in life and basically enjoy living. They don't perform their heroic deeds because they have mystical powers or the benefit of divine intervention. Their greatness comes from using their very mortal capabilities to the fullest. Like you and me, they have weaknesses and problems, but unlike us, they claim their strengths wholehearted-ly and overcome their flaws. They consciously cultivate their own abilities, expect only the best from themselves and each other, fully expect to conquer their lower impulses, and so they do.

Of course, you can't expect to merely watch *Trek* reruns and sud-denly gain Kirk's charisma. You can't throw on a Starfleet uniform, say, "Make it so," and become an instant world savior. That's okay. To be a hero doesn't mean you need to leap tall buildings or out-wit a Cardassian. Instead, you need only to pay attention to your conduct in the little events of life. Every situation, no matter how trite, offers you the opportunity to act heroically.

Think about it. Picard wows you not because he always wins, but because whatever the circumstances, he always acts with dig-nity and integrity. You *know* that Picard would somehow wash dishes in a noble manner, never complaining about the burdens of housework. He'd manage to clean toilets on the lowest deck of a Ferengi garbage scow exuding nobililty, paying close attention to detail, and certainly never complaining. He doesn't complain when his senior officer—a visiting admiral—investigates his ship and treats him with absolutely no respect in "Coming of Age." He doesn't even complain when he learns he has a degenerative dis-ease of the brain in the final episode.

That's heroism. Taking in stride whatever life offers, seeing opportunity even in misfortune, not taking problems out on oth-ers. The big victories can wait. Everyday heroism is what changes the world and changes your own consciousness.

How few of our heroes throughout history were also happy, well-rounded, kind people with virtually no interest in self-gain! There were a few, certainly. Thomas Jefferson was the best archi-tect in the United States, the best farmer in Virginia, a lawyer, inventor, philosopher, and music-lover—as well as being hand-some, brilliant, humble, and an all-around nice guy. Thomas More was a lawyer, theologian, literary scholar, statesman, and joker. "From his earliest youth he took such joy in joking that he often seemed interested in nothing else," said his friend Erasmus.

But unfortunately, such heroes of the soul, heart, mind, and body are all too few. Except, of course, aboard the *Enterprise*. There we find the best humanity has to offer embodied in each crewmember. And unlike great historical heroes, we get to watch as our *Star Trek* heroes deal with everyday problems and challenges so that we can learn from their examples.

2

RODDENBERRY'S ARK:

THE DIFFERENT TYPES OF HEROES

I look at [the Star Trek *characters] more as figures of qualities:
courage, compassion, etc. Personification of the ideal.*
—Gene Roddenberry

What makes the Tatnuck Bookseller Café in Worcester, Massachusetts, the best place on the planet for coffee and dessert? Is it the talented pastry chef, who makes Kentucky Derby Pie to die for? Or the attentive waiters, who bring whatever confection you choose to your table with prompt panache? Or the managers, who designed the all-you-can-drink coffee bar and who place a handful of books on each table for the caffeine-lover's browsing convenience—keeping the joint afloat in the cultural wasteland of Central Massachusetts?

Answer: All of the above! The talents of many people create the unique Tatnuck charm. But just imagine what would happen if they all decided to switch jobs—if the waiters decided to bake triple-chocolate torte while the pastry chef tried to balance the books. No doubt the customers would gag and our favorite café would go under.

In the same way, each *Star Trek* character makes a unique and essential contribution to the ship. Although all the characters have heroic qualities in abundance, a particular type of heroism dominates in each character. You wouldn't look to Spock for a shoulder to cry on, and you wouldn't ask Scotty to plead your case to the IRS. You wouldn't go to Worf with a medical problem, or to McCoy for physical protection. It takes many types of heroes to sustain warp drive.

In the classic episode "Mirror, Mirror," Kirk, McCoy, Uhura, and Scotty accidentally beam into a parallel universe, trading places with their counterparts from that world. They land on the deck of the *Enterprise*, but it's a mean, fascist sort of place where the resident crewmembers are violent, self-serving pirates. Each character handles the situation differently:

- Kirk immediately realizes he must adapt to his surroundings in order to survive. He assumes command of the ship and mimics the brutal behavior of his new crew. Meanwhile, he assigns tasks to Scotty, McCoy, and Uhura to buy time while he comes up with a plan.

- McCoy concentrates on the helping the people around him. When the parallel (and rather despicable) Spock gets wounded, McCoy risks his life to heal him.

- Scotty sets right to work with one-pointed determination, trying to find a way to use the power of the ship to bring the crew members back to their own universe.

- The alternate Spock, although a bad guy, does what he logically must. He analyzes the situation and realizes that he needs his own brutal captain back, and so he helps the good guys return to their own ship.

This episode beautifully illustrates how each character acts heroically, yet each in a distinctive way. All of the principal *Star Trek* characters fall into one of four categories:

Leaders, like Kirk, have a clear vision, an outstanding ability to take charge, make decisions, and implement a plan of action. Kirk, Picard, Sisko, and Janeway are Leaders.

Warriors, like Scotty, tackle problems head-on, applying exceptional focus, self-discipline—and if necessary, aggression—to get results. Worf, B'Elanna, and Kira are Warriors.

Relaters, like McCoy, express themselves freely and have great compassion and concern for others. Deanna and Lwaxana Troi, Guinan, Kes, and Bashir are also Relaters.

Analysts, like Spock, have the clear-headed, unemotional objectivity necessary to make good choices based on facts. Spock is the Analyst par excellence; Data, Tuvok, Odo, and Dax are also Analysts.

These four types of characters embody four essential aspects of the human psyche. They also reflect the four key aspects of heroism. Interestingly, the types of characters Gene Roddenberry created for the *Star Trek* universe closely parallel the personality types developed by the psychologist Carl Jung back in the early 1920s.

Jung identified a variety of "archetypes" that exist in the "collective unconscious." These archetypes have shaped myths, values, and heroic ideals in cultures around the world since the beginning of civilization. Jung's ideas about archetypes led to the belief that each person is dominated by a particular personality type that affects his or her behavior in predictable ways, in much the same way that cultural origin often affects behavior. People governed by the same personality type have many traits and aspirations in common in the same way that people with the same cultural background may share characteristics.

Many thinkers after Jung expanded on his ideas about the primary personality types and found ways to apply his findings in everyday life. For instance, they developed tests that determine personality type. Perhaps, when you applied for a new job, you had to take the Myers-Briggs Type Indicator or the Keirsey Temperament Sorter so the employer could find out if you'd "be a good fit." Recently, the Enneagram, which assesses personality using nine categories, has become a popular tool. Business people use tests like these to resolve staffing problems. Psychologists use them to better understand their patients. People who take these tests usually find the results startlingly accurate. Similarly, you can learn a lot about yourself by discovering what mix of heroic types you're made of.

The Self-Assessment Test in the next chapter will let you determine your own heroic profile. First, though, you need to know a bit more about the different heroic types.

I Am, Therefore I Am in Charge: Leaders

The leader must know, must know that he knows, and must be able to make it abundantly clear to those around him that he knows.

—Clarence B. Randall

When the Captain of the *Enterprise* says "make it so," the crew gets busy, no questions asked. All four *Star Trek* Captains—Kirk, Picard, Sisko, and Janeway—possess an aura of profound authority. Witness the way they walk: assured, in charge, knowing where they're going with every firm step. Listen to Sisko's commanding voice and take note of his steely gaze; sometimes it seems as if the only thing preventing him from ripping out your heart is the Prime Directive. Look at Picard's jutting chin and the way he puffs out his chest, or at how Janeway carries herself erect, keeping her lips pursed and maintaining a powerful stance. And Kirk moves with a confident, rolling gait; often he thrusts one shoulder forward, as if he could bulldoze his way through a brick wall. No wonder alien beings immediately figure out who the

Captain is whenever they first encounter the *Star Trek* crew.

Great leaders always have some memorable quality, in life and on *Star Trek*. This quality can be a physical characteristic, or some aspect of personality. Abe Lincoln towered over his peers, Julius Caesar had a booming voice and extraordinary energy, Napoleon was short but fierce. People with a larger-than-life presence inspire confidence in others, but it takes more than an imposing bearing to be a leader. It also takes decisiveness, purpose, and the ability to motivate others.

Like all great leaders, the *Star Trek* Captains confront problems quickly and fearlessly, make decisions easily, and always seem to know exactly what to do in times of trouble. They jump into action readily and assign tasks to others without missing a heartbeat. Although they delegate with ease, they never alienate their subordinates because they set such a good example, and they treat all with kindness and respect.

Above all, Leaders have a guiding vision that informs everything they do. *Star Trek* Captains endure repeated sacrifices for the sake of their mission. From Kirk's cry in "Arena" to his crew when facing attack, "Never mind about me. Protect the ship," to Sisko's reluctant agreement to command *Deep Space Nine* in the first episode, the *Star Trek* Leaders put aside personal comfort to do what must be done.

Real-life counterparts to these dedicated and inspiring souls appear throughout Earth's history. In this century, for instance, the labor leader Cesar Chavez organized the United Farm Workers to protest the punishing conditions that migrant workers labored under. He organized a nationwide boycott of California table grapes to secure better contracts for the workers, fighting for years against powerful establishment forces. His exceptional organizational abilities and enduring vision led to eventual victory, against all odds.

Another great contemporary Leader is Nelson Mandela, who championed the fight against the racist apartheid regime in South Africa. Although sentenced to life imprisonment in the

1960s, he continued to direct the African National Congress from his jail cell, keeping hope alive for his people and inspiring them with his quiet dignity and calm strength. And Mikhail Gorbachev, although now in disfavor, nevertheless managed to accomplish the seemingly impossible—sowing the seeds of democracy in the Soviet Union and Eastern Europe.

You'll also find Leaders in your everyday life, maybe even starting with your own family. Most families have one parent who acts as a Leader—planning the home improvements, setting the rules, determining what everyone's household duties will be. Likewise, successful business organizations usually have a Leader at the helm. If you're lucky, you have a strong Leader for a boss—someone who enjoys taking on responsibility and who encourages and inspires you. You may also have Leaders in your local government—town council members who spearhead campaigns to clean up parks or build better libraries, for instance. Such examples of leadership may not make front page news, but they are significant nonetheless.

Although measuring up to the *Star Trek* standard may seem out of your realm, you undoubtedly manifest some Leader traits, at least on occasion. Did you ever take over in a time of crisis, getting emergency medical care for a child, or keeping a dying parent hopeful? Did you ever motivate employees to work effectively in spite of their gripes with the corporation or their personal problems? Did you ever coach a sports team to victory? All these activities draw on the Leader within you.

You Are, Therefore I Challenge You: Warriors

We are going to have peace even if we have to fight for it.
—Dwight D. Eisenhower

"To die with honor" may not sound appealing compared to other activities, but to a Warrior, dying with honor ranks high among aspirations. You won't find a Warrior bumming on the beach or wearing a "Make Love Not War" T-shirt. Warriors need action.

Warriors don't seek out Rambo-type bloodfests, but they don't shrink from challenge, either. When Warriors fight, it's always for a cause they believe in. Worf, Kira, Scotty, and B'Elanna Torres will do anything in their power to defend their ships. In real life, Warriors fight injustice tirelessly, protect the helpless, and stand up for themselves and what they believe in. God help you if a Warrior is nearby when you park in a handicapped space, or carelessly toss a used tissue on the ground, or light up a cigarette in a no-smoking zone. Warriors also stand up for themselves. If you swipe a parking space from under a Warrior, you'll have a fight on your hands. Malcolm X was a Warrior; Martin Luther King was a Leader. Republicans tend toward the Warrior, fighting for lower taxes, smaller government, and, naturally, looser gun laws. Democrats, on the other hand, tend toward the Relater—"feeling the pain" of those hapless citizens the Republicans think should fend for themselves. (Unfortunately, neither party produces Leaders, except once in a blue moon.)

Warriors like hard work followed by results, and so don't retire gracefully, as Scotty demonstrates in the *Next Generation* episode "Relics." They enjoy competition and employ aggression easily, although their strong moral sense usually keeps violence and belligerence at bay. Instead, they apply discipline, persistence, and determination to tackle whatever they set their minds to. The samurai warriors of medieval Japan provide a great example, training rigorously for years to learn a strict code of ethics known as *bushido*—the warrior way. Samurai prized honor even above wealth or life. In fact, if a samurai violated the *bushido* code of honor, he atoned by committing *hara kiri*—unflinching ritual suicide.

Although the days of the samurai are long gone, the Warrior's spirit still thrives on Earth. Athletes routinely learn to respond like Warriors in their training, as do sales people, managers, and of course, people in the military. To succeed, these professionals need to know how to focus and how to anticipate and fend off moves. You can't play sports if you can't concentrate or anticipate reactions; nor can you sell cars or manage projects without these strengths. Warriors across the professional spectrum also need agility, endurance, and assertiveness—and the intelligence to use these qualities properly. And it doesn't hurt to have a generous dose of loyalty, a profound sense of duty, and even a willingness to die for the cause.

Warriors don't show up only in competitive arenas, though. Mothers who go to the school board to demand special services for their children act like Warriors. So do students who challenge a remark by a formidable professor, consumers who take on companies that sell shoddy products, even people who muster fortitude in order to endure a trip to the dentist.

If you consider yourself too gentle a soul to have Warrior traits, think again. Although you may not have what it takes to be the *Enterprise* Security Officer, you've certainly invoked your inner Warrior on occasion. Did you ever fight with a store clerk to take back defective merchandise? Did you ever contest an unfair bill or parking ticket, or return poorly prepared food in a restaurant? Did you ever point out to someone that he just made a bigoted or sexist remark? All these actions rely on the Warrior within you.

You Are, Therefore I'll Take Care of You: Relaters

> *Nothing makes me more happy than to render any service in my power, of whatsoever description.*
>
> —Thomas Jefferson

You can spot a Relater in two seconds at any party. Look for the person having the most fun, in the most public way. Or at a meeting, find a Relater by looking for the person who worries more about "how all this will affect so-and-so" than about getting business done. Relaters bring people together, settle arguments, and possess a remarkable ability to understand and empathize with all living beings. They draw on this gift to recognize others' need and to understand their motivations, and to shower the people in their lives with compassion.

Relaters let their hearts lead. In the *Next Generation* episode "Ensign Ro," Guinan transforms a violently hostile Bajoran into a friend by persistently reaching out to her when others turn away. Guinan lives to give, and her job as bartender lets her do just that. Like most Relaters, she has foolproof intuition, and so crew members flock to her for wise counsel when logic fails them. She shows her compassion again in "The Offspring," when she hires Data's daughter, Lal, to help tend bar. Not that she really needs the help: She just wants Lal to have a chance to socialize. Like Lal, we sure could benefit from having someone with Guinan's kindness in our own lives: a mentor at work who spends extra time showing us the ropes; a friend who always seems to know the right thing to say; a doctor who listens carefully to our complaints without automatically pushing a pill our way.

True Relaters know how to play and have fun. They love life, and approach everything with enthusiasm. They care for all living things, and will sacrifice themselves to serve others. In the *Deep Space Nine* episode "The Forsaken," Lwaxana Troi manages to melt the icy heart of Odo—a seemingly impossible feat—by showering him with relentless affection and empathy and finally revealing her own vulnerability to him.

Jesus Christ was the ultimate Relater, teaching people to love each other, treat each other with kindness, and forgive each other no matter what. His overflowing love for humanity prompted him to beg God to forgive even the people who led him to his death. Like Christ, most great spiritual figures have Relater personalities; so do humanitarians who work in the trenches to uplift and heal the suffering. Albert Schweitzer, for example, went to French Equatorial Africa (now Gabon) in 1913 to serve as a medical missionary. He established hospitals there and treated thousands for leprosy and other diseases. He also wrote books putting

forth his philosophy of "reverence for life," which stresses mutual respect and compassion for all living things. Fortunately,
Schweitzer's efforts were rewarded with the Nobel Peace Prize in
1952.

Like Schweitzer and even like Christ, you surely have *some*
Relater traits within you, although you may not have Lwaxana's
steamroller gregariousness. Whenever you try to put a shy person
at ease, when you forgive someone who wronged you, when you
go out of your way for a friend just for the joy of giving (expecting
nothing in return), when you jump in a pile of leaves or dance
crazy out of sheer exuberance, your inner Relater is the force that
moves you. If you get a little choked up watching a romantic
movie or listening to a Beethoven symphony (or even seeing a nos-
talgic Hallmark card ad), that's the Relater in you coming to the
fore. The Relater manifests in the thrill of joy you feel when you
hear about another person's success; in your desire to heal a child's
broken heart. It's what makes you shiver with delight when you
see a rainbow or a magnificent sunset.

I Think, Therefore I Am: Analysts

> *You know my method. It is founded upon the observance of trifles.*
>
> —Sherlock Holmes (a.k.a. Arthur Conan Doyle)

Analysts embody logic and reason. They love facts and pay great
attention to detail. While Relaters show us the *subjective* point of
view, Analysts keep us in touch with more *objective* reality.

Spock is the ultimate Analyst. In the episode "Errand of Mercy,"
the *Enterprise* crew fights a nasty battle on a hostile planet. Kirk asks
Spock their odds of survival. Spock replies: "Difficult to be precise,
Captain. I should say approximately 7,824.7 to 1." Raising his point-
ed eyebrow, Spock adds solemnly, "I endeavor to be accurate."

Analysts don't tolerate sloppy thinking or conjecture. Their devotion to facts and reason leaves little room for emotion, even in the

face of death. Spock sacrifices his own life in *The Wrath of Khan* because it's the "logical thing to do." He occasionally alienates others by bluntly reciting his observations about them, as in "The Alternative Factor," when he says to Lazarus, "I fail to comprehend your indignation, sir. I have simply made the logical deduction that you are a liar." Analysts see the cold, hard truth and speak it freely.

The honor student who can't get a date, the mad scientist who forgets to bathe—these are Analysts gone overboard. Analysts can easily become nerds, but at their best, they quietly save the day with their brilliant thinking and encyclopedic knowledge. Data knows the facts about literally everything in the universe; when Picard gets in trouble in the final episode of *The Next Generation*, he turns to Data, the only crewmember capable of understanding the complexities of his dilemma. Again and again, Data, Dax, Tuvok, and Spock offer brilliant solutions to so-called impossible problems by applying incisive, clearsighted, and objective analysis.

Although Analysts play a pivotal role in the *Star Trek* universe, here on Earth, they rarely make front-page news. Unlike Leaders, Analysts don't relish the spotlight. Instead, they experiment and investigate and question everything, seeking the truth. And like Sherlock Holmes—who Data reveres—they usually find it. Analysts often are unsung heroes behind other people's achievements. They're the experts in the crime labs who run the DNA tests that nail criminals, while the prosecuting attorneys grab the limelight and the glory. They're the statisticians and researchers who feed sports announcers those incredible factoids that make them seem like all-knowing sages. They're the copyeditors who fix an author's prose to keep the critics from howling in derision at some grammatical faux pas.

You'll find many Analysts working in the sciences, where they can pursue their love of facts and orderly process. People like Einstein, Thomas Edison, and John Gibbon, who invented the heart-lung machine, provide great examples. They all worked relentlessly to gather facts, synthesize information, test their theories, and make breakthrough discoveries. Gibbon spent decades attempting to perfect the heart-lung machine before it could be released. Finally, in the 1950s, it was first used successfully in humans, ushering in the modern era of cardiac surgery. More recently, Stephen Hawking wrote *A Brief History of Time*, presenting his brilliant work in theoretical physics, accomplished despite an incurable disease that renders him unable to move, turn the pages of a book, or even speak without the aid of a computer.

Do you have Analyst traits? Yes, if you enjoy taking things apart to see how they work. Yes, if you work with your money management program for more than two hours a night. Yes, if you keep your mouth shut at work when your boss angers you because you want a promotion and can assess the consequences of taking rash action. The Analyst within keeps you solvent and out of jail.

Can Leaders Love and Lovers Lead?

Deep within, we all possess all four of the heroic types—Leader, Warrior, Analyst, Relater—to some degree. In fact, the greatest heroes develop and maintain all of these heroic aspects and hold them in balance. That balance can—must—shift as circumstances change. At one stage of a task, for example, you may need your Analyst traits to get a realistic picture of your situation and what lies ahead. But once you finish your assessment, you may need to call on your Warrior aspect to take action and get the job done.

Achieving appropriate balance isn't easy. When people have an excess of one trait and not enough of another to offset it, there's a danger that they'll become maniacs or misfits: Too much of a good thing can turn heroes into heels. What makes Saddam Hussein despicable? The fact that he's all Warrior, with not enough Relater. Likewise, Relaters who lack Warrior or Leader traits can end up in hot water. Bill "I Feel Your Pain" Clinton, for instance, charmed the American public into electing him, happily surrounding himself with fans and friends from coast to coast.

Unfortunately, his joie de vivre wore thin when he failed to muster enough Leader to take charge in the White House.

In *Star Trek*, circumstances often force the characters to develop other qualities. In the *Next Generation* episode "Disaster," for instance, Troi finds herself in charge of the Bridge, faced with the need to make life-and-death decisions. At first, she balks—leadership does not come easily to her—but she finally rises to the occasion. Meanwhile, Picard gets trapped in an elevator with a group of children, his worst nightmare. Somehow, he overcomes kidphobia, mustering enough Relater to console the frightened tykes. We frequently face similar challenges in our own lives, needing to act like a Warrior in order to get a promotion at work in spite of our desire to withdraw completely, for instance; or needing to learn how to act like an Analyst in order to assess our household finances, although our natural inclination is to spend lavishly.

We often fail to follow the right path for our temperament simply because we don't recognize our own heroic profile. We don't have a good picture of our own strengths and weaknesses; even worse, we don't believe in our own potential. Perhaps at some crucial point in your life you attempted to act like a Leader but didn't achieve your aim. Then you felt shamed and put your Leader uniform in mothballs. Or you set out to be a Warrior but suffered such deep and painful wounds that you let your sword rust from disuse. Young boys learn not to cry or display Relater traits; girls learn not to act aggressive. Such teachings, delivered in the wrong way at the wrong time, trample the budding heroic psyche.

Every person has heroic qualities, but those qualities must be cultivated in order to become obvious. Identifying your own heroic type and bringing forward your innate heroic qualities will help you to make wise decisions about your life. If you find that you have mostly Relater traits, you might want to reconsider your plan to earn an MBA and explore careers in social work or the arts instead. A Warrior? Drop out of Library School pronto. A Leader? Quit that accounting job and start your own business.

On the other hand, you might find that you have *overdeveloped* your predominant heroic type, neglecting other aspects of your being. We contain all the heroic qualities within us, but we tend to let one set of traits dominate while completely ignoring others. For example, you can easily manifest your Warrior to get the task done but can't sustain a relationship (weak Relater). Or you do well in love but get stepped on at work (weak Warrior). All of your heroic traits must awaken or you risk becoming mentally, physically, and spiritually unbalanced.

What makes Spock so appealing? It's the hint of Relater that occasionally shows beneath his Analyst veneer. Picard the Leader has a strong Analyst bent and acts like a Warrior when he needs to. The *Star Trek* characters exemplify a balance of heroic traits. They manifest their unique heroic types while still displaying other heroic qualities.

The Self-Assessment Test in the next chapter will help you to identify your own heroic type and bring to the fore all your heroic qualities.

3

ARE YOU A WORF, SPOCK, GUINAN, OR KIRK?

THE SELF-ASSESSMENT TEST

The Self-Assessment Test on the next several pages will help you to discover which *Star Trek* characters you resemble most closely and which you need to learn from. Do you require more Worf so that bullies don't take advantage of you, or more Guinan so that you don't take advantage of everyone else? Are you a budding Picard or Kirk just waiting for a worthy mission? Turn to page 38 for detailed instructions about how to interpret your score.

For each multiple choice question below, choose the response that most closely represents your preferences or typical behaviors, and circle the symbol to the left of it (✳, ▲, ●, or ✚). Choose only one response for each question. If none of the responses match your preferences (or if several do), please choose the best available response. A few of the questions contain esoteric *Star Trek* popular culture references. If you don't know any of the items listed, go on to the next question.

1. **Which videos would you rent after a hard day at work if these were your only choices:**

   * *Moonstruck* and *Big*
   ▲ *Presumed Innocent* and *The Client*
   ● *Gandhi* and *Dead Poets Society*
   ✚ *Die Hard* and *The Terminator*

2. **The perfect mate for you:**

   ● is determined to make the world a better place
   ▲ is organized and realistic
   * is affectionate and has a great sense of humor
   ✚ is energetic and speaks his or her mind

3. **If Q granted you one of these wishes, which would you opt for?**

   * making everyone around you (including yourself) permanently happy
   ✚ smashing the previous sprint record at the Olympics
   ● getting elected President, wiping out the deficit, and restoring pride in the nation
   ▲ I would refuse to make a wish until Q revealed his motives.

4. **I prefer parties:**

   * where I can actually converse
   ✚ that include activities like volleyball, softball, ultimate frisbee
   ● that give me a chance to network
   ▲ that I can avoid

5. **Which comic strip would you rather read?**
   ▲ "Zippy the Pinhead"
   * "Calvin & Hobbes"
   ● A cartoon by Szep
   ✚ "Batman"

6. **If I had a four-day vacation, I'd:**

   ● charter my own boat and take out my family or friends
   ✳ go to Disneyland
   ✚ work straight through it if I had a pressing project due
   ▲ go to a *Star Trek* convention

7. **After getting stopped by a police officer for doing 65 in a 55-m.p.h. zone, I'd most likely:**

   ✳ try to butter him up and act real friendly
   ▲ take a deep breath and consider various options before reacting
   ● inform him that I was on my way to an important meeting, and see if we could negotiate a settlement
   ✚ challenge the accuracy of his radar gun

8. **I'd prefer to play:**

   ✳ Twister
   ▲ Trivial Pursuit
   ● Monopoly
   ✚ Darts

9. **Imagine that a strange planet is about to explode, but the Prime Directive forbids you from interfering with the doomed civilization on the planet. Suddenly you pick up a desperate radio hail from a little girl on the planet. Your next move is to:**

   ▲ ask the computer if a precedent for interference exists in such dire situations
   ● report the hail to the Captain
   ✳ respond, despite the Prime Directive
   ✚ confront the Captain about doing something to rescue the girl

10. **With a Romulan warbird approaching, my first reaction would be to:**

    ●   gather my chief officers together to devise a strategy and assign tasks

    ✚   raise shields and arm torpedoes

    ✳   try to make friendly contact with the Romulan ship

    ▲   quickly review the available data on current relations with Romulans

11. **The best Christmas present for me would be:**

    ✳   a Golden Retriever puppy

    ▲   a new laptop with CD-ROM

    ●   a sizeable donation in my name to help Haitian refugees

    ✚   tickets to the Super Bowl

12. **At 9:00 P.M., I'd rather be:**

    ✚   exercising vigorously

    ✳   talking on the phone to a friend

    ▲   hacking on my computer

    ●   organizing my schedule for the next day

13. **Who would you most want to lunch with?**

    ✳   Oprah Winfrey and Leo Buscaglia

    ▲   Margaret Mead and Carl Sagan

    ●   Margaret Thatcher and Nelson Mandela

    ✚   Hillary Clinton and General Schwarzkopf

14. **Which post would you opt for on the *Enterpise?***

    ✳   Ship's Counselor

    ●   Captain

    ✚   Chief of Security

    ▲   Science Officer

15. **I'd like to be reborn as:**

- ● Thomas Jefferson
- ✚ Napoleon
- ✳ Don Juan
- ▲ Madame Curie

16. **I'd rather drive:**

- ● a Cadillac Eldorado
- ✚ a Mazda Miata
- ✳ a Dodge Caravan
- ▲ It depends on many factors, such as selling price, this year's crash test results, and the options available for the particular vehicle.

17. **The worst thing that could happen to me would be to:**

- ▲ lose my ability to reason
- ✳ lose my inner joy
- ● lose my sense of purpose
- ✚ lose my self-confidence

18. **In *The Wizard of Oz*, I would like to be:**

- ✳ The Scarecrow
- ▲ The Tin Man
- ● Dorothy
- ✚ The Lion

19. **If my boss seemed in a lousy mood and snapped at me:**

- ✳ I'd ask her if she felt okay.
- ▲ I'd avoid her and do my work.
- ● I'd try to take some of the pressure off of her.
- ✚ I'd let her know that I don't appreciate being yelled at.

20. **I'd rather teach:**

   ● American government
   ✚ labor relations
   ✳ clinical social work
   ▲ advanced calculus

21. **If I got stuck on a desert island and could only have one book, I'd choose:**

   ▲ an almanac
   ● *The Seven Habits of Highly Effective People,* by Stephen R. Covey
   ✚ *Swim with the Sharks,* by Harvey Mackay
   ✳ *The Road Less Traveled,* by M. Scott Peck

22. **If I had to change careers, I'd rather be a:**

   ✳ talk show host
   ▲ research biochemist
   ● university president
   ✚ trial lawyer

23. **Which TV show would you prefer a leading role in?**

   ✳ *Seinfeld*
   ✚ *Rescue 911*
   ▲ *Mystery!*
   ● *Eye to Eye with _____* (your name)

24. **If I got stranded alone on a distant asteroid, with no hope of escape, the worst problem for me would be:**

   ▲ having nothing to occupy my mind; boredom
   ● having no sense of purpose; resignation
   ✳ having nobody to talk to; loneliness
   ✚ I'd find a way to escape.

25. **If a thirteen-year-old kid tried to steal my wallet, I'd:**

   ✳ call his parents and make sure they got him counseling
   ▲ ask him what motivated him to do it
   ● lecture him sternly and hope he learns a lesson
   ✚ grab him by the collar and call the cops

26. **If my boss gave me one day to complete a three-day project, I'd:**

   ✳ eat sweets, drink coffee, and do my best in the one-day period
   ● recruit people to help me out
   ✚ tell my boss right away that her expectations are unreasonable
   ▲ determine exactly what I could accomplish in one day and communicate to my boss the need for more time

27. **On Saturday morning, I'd rather:**

   ● coach Little League or organize a group outing
   ▲ read Roger Zelazny's *Amber* series
   ✚ take a martial arts class
   ✳ talk to friends and family on the phone

28. **I'd prefer to watch:**

   ● *Picket Fences*
   ✳ *Oprah*
   ▲ *Face the Nation*
   ✚ *Murphy Brown*

29. **I'd prefer to listen to:**

   ✚ Van Halen
   ✳ Yanni
   ▲ Frank Zappa
   ● Bruce Springsteen

30. **When somebody I know gets sick, I:**

   *   enjoy visiting her to cheer her up
   ▲   stay away, particularly if she's contagious
   ●   bring her interesting things to work on or read
   ✚   encourage her to stay active

31. **When the conversation turns political, I:**

   ✚   usually get angry and insult someone
   *   try to redirect it back to more enjoyable topics
   ▲   make certain I back up whatever I say with facts
   ●   become animated and engaged in the discussion

32. **If elected President, the first thing I'd do would be to:**

   ✚   get to work on restoring the nation's position as a super-
   power
   *   work on social problems like drug abuse and poverty
   ▲   I would never run for President in the first place.
   ●   recruit and train competent advisers

33. **My dog or cat should first and foremost be:**

   ●   independent
   ▲   highly intelligent
   ✚   obedient
   *   cute and fuzzy

34. **When my computer crashes, I:**

   ✚   have a fit, then figure out what to do
   *   call a friend for advice
   ▲   figure out what caused the crash
   ●   hire a skilled technician to repair it

35. *Star Trek* is primarily a show about:

   ✳ people who are inspiring
   ▲ interesting possibilities for humanity's future
   ● maintaining the highest values and principles
   ✚ great special effects

36. If Neelix cooked a feast for me and asked how I liked a dish that I hated, I'd:

   ▲ ask what ingredients he used so I could figure out what went wrong
   ✳ tell him it's delicious to spare his feelings
   ✚ answer honestly, telling him straight out that I didn't like it
   ● find a diplomatic way to avoid responding at all

37. My former dates would say I'm:

   ▲ logical
   ● principled
   ✚ assertive
   ✳ romantic

38. My favorite Muppet is:

   ▲ Scooter
   ● Kermit
   ✚ Miss Piggy
   ✳ Gonzo

39. When I feel blue, I:

   ▲ withdraw
   ✳ talk to a friend about it
   ● force myself to be productive
   ✚ I don't allow myself to get blue.

40. I prefer clothing that is:

✳ dramatic and fun
● conservative and expensive
✚ comfortable and easy to move in
▲ trendy and reasonably priced

SCORING YOUR ASSESSMENT

Count the circled symbols on the previous pages.

Totals: ✳'s _____(RELATER)

▲'s _____(ANALYST)

●'s _____(LEADER)

✚'s _____(WARRIOR)

Highest Score   _____

Second Highest Score   _____

Third Highest Score   _____

Lowest Score   _____

ABOUT YOUR SCORE

■ The highest score shows your main heroic type.

■ The lowest score shows your weakest heroic aspect.

■ If you scored over 7 for any heroic type, you have developed the traits for that type to a sufficient degree. The higher your score, the more completely you have integrated the characteristics of that type into your psyche *and* behavior.

■ If you scored under 7 for any of the heroic types, you need to develop that aspect of your personality. A score of under 7 indicates an area that may cause you trouble. The lower the score, the more problems this area might pose for you.

■ It is quite common to score the same number in two or more heroic aspects. The sample results on the next few pages should help you to interpret a tied score.

■ What is an ideal score? Ideally, you want to score quite high in all of the aspects—13 or more in your primary heroic aspect, and at least 7 in each of the others. Higher scores in all of the aspects show that you have access to all of your inner heroes. Although most people have work to do before achieving this goal, the exercises in this book will definitely help.

The sample test results on the following pages will help you to understand more specifically what your score means.

Sample Self-Assessment Test Results #1:
A RELATER PROFILE

SCORE: 18   Relater
          9   Warrior
          8   Analyst
          5   Leader

INTERPRETATION: This person loves to hang out and socialize. With a very high Relater score of 18, he'd be a good person to tell your darkest secrets to, to lean on in times of trouble, to keep as your friend. Because he has a reasonably strong Warrior with a score of 9, he manages to take care of his *own* needs as well as those of others. He's the kind of friend who lets you know he loves you, but also lets you know when he thinks you need to change. His low Leader score indicates little interest in planning ahead. He tends toward impulsive behavior, living for the moment. He certainly doesn't grab power, and might actually refuse responsibility inappropriately.

CONCLUSION: Like Peter Pan, this person is a lot of fun, but you may find yourself occasionally wishing that he'd grow up a little.

Sample Self-Assessment Test Results #2:
A WARRIOR PROFILE

SCORE: 19 Warrior
              13 Leader
               5 Analyst
               3 Relater

INTERPRETATION: This person has no problem asking for a raise or confronting overly loud neighbors. With a Warrior score of 19, she stands up for what she believes in and asserts herself when necessary. She also has a reasonably high score for Leader and a very low score for Relater. This indicates a person who likes to take charge but who unfortunately doesn't pay much attention to the feelings of people under her. She may not listen well, but does a great job of letting others know her own wants, needs, and priorities. The high Warrior/Leader combined with very low Relater could make this person very difficult to get along with. She also has a relatively low Analyst score, which indicates that she might speak inappropriately before thinking through the consequences.

CONCLUSION: Avoid confrontations with this person at all costs.

Sample Self-Assessment Test Results #3:
A LEADER PROFILE

SCORE: 16 Leader
              12 Relater
               7 Warrior
               5 Analyst

INTERPRETATION: This person would make a great boss. With a high Leader score of 16, he likes to take on responsibility, and has a strong sense of mission. Fortunately, his very high Relater score makes him a compassionate manager who encourages others and respects their values, even when their values don't support his cause. He has just enough Warrior to see things through to completion and to speak directly to people when problems arise. The low Analyst score is the only problem area. He tends to act on impulse, letting his enthusiasm for his mission carry him away—and sometimes creates problems by overlooking details and neglecting the facts.

CONCLUSION: Do whatever you can to get on this person's team—but be prepared to shoulder the burden of doing the detail work and keeping plans grounded in reality.

Sample Self-Assessment Test Results #4:
AN ANALYST PROFILE

SCORE: 18 Analyst
          13 Warrior
           6 Leader
           3 Relater

INTERPRETATION: This person is thorough, hard-working, detail-oriented, and able to complete the most complex, demanding jobs. Her very high Analyst score of 18 means she hardly ever gets sloppy, resists jumping to conclusions, and she keeps her emotions in check. Although she may do well in jobs requiring independent research, her very low Relater score of 3, combined with the high Warrior score of 13, could make her difficult to work with. She prefers solitary jobs, makes little effort to put others at ease, and in fact, may alienate people with tactless comments. Unfortunately, her underdeveloped social skills may even cause her to sabotage her brilliant accomplishments by aggravating the people she reports to.

CONCLUSION: If you need an outside consultant to do any sort of evaluation, hire this woman.

Sample Self-Assessment Test Results #5:
A WELL-ROUNDED HEROIC PROFILE

SCORE: 11 Leader
              11 Relater
               9 Warrior
               9 Analyst

INTERPRETATION: This person seems at first look to have inner balance, with all the scores almost equal. She probably presents an image to the world of being a decent, sane human being. With a Relater of 11, she knows how to play and treats other people well; with a Leader of 11, she can take charge when necessary; her Analyst of 9 gives her some ability to make rational decisions and control her emotions; and her Warrior of 9 ensures that she asserts herself on occasion. Unfortunately, although she has no areas of extreme weakness, she also has no areas of great strength. This could actually make her personality a bit flat. She needs to practice the exercises for developing all the inner heroes.

CONCLUSION: This is the kind of person you *should* fall in love with, but somehow the chemistry is never there. Nevertheless, she's honest and loyal, so give her a chance, at least as a friend.

PART TWO

SWAGGER BOLDLY AND CARRY A BIG

PHASER: LIFE LESSONS FROM THE

WARRIORS, WORF, KIRA,

B'ELANNA, AND SCOTTY

4

NO TEARS, NO FEARS, AND A SPEEDY

TRIGGER FINGER: THE WARRIOR'S CREDO

I'm not the greatest; I'm the double greatest. Not only do I knock 'em out, I pick the round.

—Muhammad Ali

In "The Icarus Factor," Worf aches to go through a Klingon rite of passage to prove his worth as a warrior. The ceremony requires him to endure tremendous physical suffering without flinching: He must walk a path lined by Klingons who brutally stab him with pain sticks. Worf takes it like a Klingon, proudly announcing, "Today I am a warrior. I travel the river of blood." Finally, he collapses on the floor, writhing in agony.

Worf vividly embodies the fortitude, stamina, and willingness to sacrifice that constitute the true Warrior spirit. Not that Warriors crave torture: They aren't mere brutes, roaming the galaxy looking for fights and beating up on weaker souls. When Warriors take up sword and shield, it's always for an honorable cause.

Righteous indignation is what fuels the Warrior. To defend the cause, Warriors will do anything, although they adhere to a strict code of honor in all behavior. Aggression without a good reason is unforgivable to a Warrior: Honor always comes first.

Here's a great story that illustrates just how important honor is to Warriors. It's from the book *King, Warrior, Magician, Lover*, by Robert Moore and Douglas Gillette: In medieval Japan, there was a samurai warrior whose lord was murdered by a rival. The samurai swore to avenge the murder, and so he tracked the killer for many years, enduring great personal sacrifice and hardship. At last he found the villain, cornered him, and drew his sword. Just then, however, the murderer spat into his face. Instead of attacking the murderer, the samurai put away his sword, turned on his heels, and walked away.

Why did the samurai split the scene? Because honor demanded that he fight *only* on behalf of his lord and master. If he attacked the murderer after the spitting incident, he would have acted out of personal anger—not out of loyalty to his lord—thus betraying his samurai oath and compromising the honor of the Warrior clan. Honor, the story tells us, means fighting for a cause, not for personal gain.

Like the samurai, the *Star Trek* Warriors fight only when a noble cause presents itself—but then they scrap with great gusto. For instance, in the *Deep Space Nine* episode "Duet," Kira ruthlessly bares her fangs and goes after a Cardassian war criminal. Her aggressive stance comes from her heartfelt conviction that the Cardassian committed unforgivable horrors against innocent Bajoran people and therefore must be punished. She pursues her victim with a Warrior's vengeance—not for personal glory, but because she seeks retribution for her people.

Numerous real-life Warriors throughout history have shown as much eagerness to fight tooth-and-nail for a cause as Kira does. For instance, Susan B. Anthony, who spent half a century campaigning for the rights of women and black people. She began her work to reform laws that discriminated against women in 1851. She published a newspaper on women's issues and spent the rest of her life agitating for a constitutional amendment granting women the right to vote. She also worked tirelessly for the emancipation of the slaves, protesting the violence directed against blacks and lobbying for the participation of blacks in the women's suffrage movement. Fourteen years after her death, in 1920, the Nineteenth Amendment finally passed, giving women the right to vote.

In this century, Rosa Parks, a black seamstress, housekeeper, and ordinary member of the community, suddenly decided not to give up her seat on an Alabama bus to a white person in 1956. She stood her ground with a Warrior's conviction, got arrested for violating segregation laws, and kicked off the boycott of the Montgomery bus system that Martin Luther King ultimately led. The boycott became a turning point in the civil rights movement and finally led to desegregation. By refusing to budge, this woman demonstrated the true Warrior spirit.

If you look around, you'll find numerous other so-called ordinary people turned into Warriors fighting for what they believe in: the volunteers who go door-to-door collecting funds on behalf of Greenpeace and speaking out against environmental injustice; the members of Mothers Against Drunk Driving (MADD), who campaign tirelessly to raise the drinking age, impose stiffer penalties for alcohol-impaired drivers, and reduce accessibility of alcohol to teenagers. Consider the New Jersey couple who, after the rape and death of their seven-year-old daughter at the hands of a twice-convicted sex offender, lobbied to pass a law ensuring that residents are notified if a known sexual offender lives in their neighborhood. People like these embody the Warrior spirit.

Warriors don't knot up inside debating with themselves about what deserves retribution and what does not. They see the world in black and white and react swiftly to anything that violates their moral code. If speaking out and taking up arms gets the Warrior in serious trouble, so be it: To a Warrior, dying with honor is the ultimate achievement. In fact, among certain Native American cultures, Warriors greeted each dawn by saying, "Today is a good day to die!"—also a favorite Klingon greeting.

It's not that Warriors crave death, but if death comes, they'll be ready for it. The Warriors' readiness to meet death at any moment heightens their awareness to the nth degree, awakens their senses, and makes every moment of life rich and full.

A classic story about a Zen monk beautifully illustrates this point. The monk fell over a cliff, but managed to grasp a root and prevented himself from falling. As he dangled there, he looked up and noticed a mouse nibbling on the root. Looking down, he saw a hungry tiger pacing below, licking her lips in anticipation of her next meal. Just then he noticed a luscious berry growing on the side of the cliff. The monk picked the berry and placed it in his mouth. "How sweet it tastes!" he cried. Now, *that's* a War-rior—fully alive and living in the moment, although suspended above the jaws of death.

Of course, simply developing a samurai attitude won't make you a Warrior. Warriors also have one-pointed determination; they don't give up until they attain their goal. This quality of relent-lessness drives Warriors to achieve remarkable things, although sometimes at tremendous personal cost. It's relentlessness, more than anything else, that sets Warriors apart from the rest of us. The Warrior is the one who brazenly speaks out while others politely stifle; who keeps harping on some point of contention until every-body else caves in. When the rest of the crowd backs down to keep the peace, the Warrior storms ahead, unafraid.

Many of history's great Warriors won their unlikely victories by persisting even in the face of overwhelming odds. Before the battle of Agincourt, Henry V did a little calculating and figured out that there were five French soldiers for every one of his own. Did he call for reinforcements? Not on his life. Instead he delight-ed in the fact that he had so few soldiers; more than enough Eng-lishmen, he said, to get the job done, but few enough so that each would have a huge share of the glory to come.

No wonder the wimps among us fear Warriors! If a Warrior thinks you did something wrong, you'll hear about it within five seconds. No little white lies, no trumped-up stories to spare your feelings. Whatever a Warrior feels gets expressed.

In the *Voyager* episode "Parallax," Captain Janeway interviews B'Elanna for a post as Chief Engineer. When asked some hard questions about her past, B'Elanna blurts out, "I didn't want to have anything to do with Starfleet then, and I'm sorry I have to now!" Likewise, when Worf's brother gets invited to a banquet aboard the *Enterprise*, he loudly criticizes the food, proclaiming it bland and tasteless. Warriors don't play diplomacy games, even to get what they want.

Warriors often triumph simply because others don't want to confront them. Who wants to take on a foe who prizes the truth above good relations; who isn't afraid to say *anything*, no matter what the cost? In fact, not everyone appreciates the Warrior's blunt style. Look at what happened to Jocelyn Elders, Bill Clinton's former surgeon general. She said exactly what she thought about sex education with little regard for public opinion, and ended up losing her post. Had Clinton acted more like a Warrior himself, he might have defended his appointee.

Unlike the unfortunate Ms. Elders, most Warriors get their point across one way or another, wielding pen as well as sword, if necessary. Martin Luther, for instance, infuriated the Catholic establishment by writing down the ninety-five things that bugged him about the way religion had become perverted and nailing the list to the door of a church. Vaclav Havel of Czechoslovakia satirized the Communist regime in his plays, continuing to speak out for human rights even after his plays were banned and he was imprisoned. He inspired public protests that ultimately led to the fall of the regime. Like Luther and Havel, Warriors rarely cave in without a rip-roaring fight. You might want to run for your life if a Warrior decides to take *you* on, but kiss the ground in gratitude if a Warrior takes your side.

If you think Warriors should learn to mince words and mind their manners, think again. Without Warriors, evolution would screech to a halt. Every successful organization on the planet needs at least one Warrior in the ranks preventing stagnation, bucking the odds so that dreams can become realities. The P.T.A. Warrior pushes hard for school reform; the Warrior in the factory organizes a strike; the Warrior in the classroom challenges the ill-prepared teacher; the Warrior in government takes on big business.

Warriors have a driving will that others lack—a need for completion, an inability to repress their impulses simply to preserve appearances. If you want to drive a Warrior nuts, try making small talk. Warriors like to take action, not discuss. A Warrior will be at the battlefront ready for combat before you even figure out where the battlefront is.

You probably know someone who always finds a good and righteous reason to get outraged. Like a dog sniffing the kitchen floor for crumbs, Warriors have a talent for finding the things in life that need cleaning up. When they run out of issues to pursue, they become as pesky and grumpy as hungry mutts.

For instance, Scotty turns snarly in the *Next Generation* episode "Relics" because he can't adjust to retired life. In "A Fistful of Datas," Worf pooh-poohs his shipmates who spend so much time in the holodeck, scoffing at their interest in playing shoot-'em-up in a simulated Western town. But when the fighting begins and he gets a chance to bash a few heads, he grins a deep Klingon grin and begins to see that the holodeck might have some virtues after all.

Of course, Warriors come in many varieties—in *Star Trek* and in real life. For instance, Scotty displays some Warrior characteristics, but not others. Like a Warrior, he never fritters away time chit-chatting with his crewmates. He relentlessly works to keep the *Enterprise* running, showing Warrior-like fortitude even under dire conditions. He focuses completely on the task before him, bluntly speaks his mind, and never procrastinates. Scotty also has some of the combat-ready edginess of B'Elanna, Kira, and Worf. He'll risk his life to defend the object of his devotion— usually the *Enterprise*. He will *not* tolerate slurs against his first love. In "The Trouble with Tribbles," he sits on his temper while a Klingon rabble-rouser hurls insults against the Federation,

Kirk, and almost everyone else in the galaxy. But when the Klingon calls the *Enterprise* a "sagging old rust-bucket," Scotty flies into a rage and instigates a barroom brawl.

Scotty isn't usually so anxious to fight or even to exert himself. With his slight beer belly and graying temples, he knows he's not exactly a physical dynamo. For that matter, he doesn't seem to enjoy verbal combat much either, preferring to bury himself in his work.

Worf, on the other hand, toughens himself up at every opportunity. Prizing his skill in Klingon martial arts, he teaches self-defense in his spare time. And when he feels violated or threatened, you can count on him for a quick show of hurricane-force might. In "Sins of the Father," Worf's brother Kurn accuses him of turning soft. No greater insult could fall on Worf's ears. In an instant, he's hurling a chair at Kurn, boasting that he'll happily give a demonstration of his fighting skill at a moment's notice.

In spite of Worf's great power, only his enemies need fear him. With his Starfleet friends, he is Mr. Protocol, always displaying exemplary behavior. He manages to control his temper to comply with the Federation code of ethics; when his compatriots irritate him, he just growls under his breath and holds his phaser in check.

How do Worf and Scotty and the other *Star Trek* Warriors correspond to real-life people you know?

Scotty is the kind of guy you find still at work at 3:00 A.M., not because he wants to earn brownie points, but because some problem remains unresolved. He wouldn't think of calling in sick, even if he had a fever approximating the temperature of the surface of Mercury and was tossing his cookies with the ferocity of a volcano on Jupiter's moon Io. Warriors of Scotty's type excel at their jobs, show amazing stamina, get anxious during slow times, have no patience with people who get in their way, and speak bluntly (even tactlessly) about matters at hand. You see a Scotty climbing a utility pole at 3:00 A.M. in the middle of a torrential downpour to fix the power lines. Or you observe her in the operating room conducting a multi-organ transplant on a four-year-old child, after a twenty-four-hour shift, barking out orders to the residents and nurses around her.

Real-life Worfs are the strong, silent types; those who "walk softly but carry a big stick." They know the value of physical discipline—practicing Tae Kwon Do, weightlifting, or some other demanding sport. They have a lean, mean look and on occasion may demolish their foes—whether on the squash court or in a corporate meeting room—yet they treat all with exemplary courtesy. They quietly sacrifice their own desires for whatever cause they decide to adopt, showing great nobility of character. Still, they ooze a steamy power that you feel seething under the surface, and so you instinctively think twice before taking them on.

B'Elanna and Kira, on the other hand, have fire in their lungs. They use their words like whips when angered, and have no trouble using fists as well. Both have hair-trigger tempers (and often carry big grudges), both speak their minds at the drop of a tricorder, and both are brilliant tacticians. Barbra Streisand offers an Earthly counterpart to B'Elanna. Both her bell-like singing and her outspokenness on behalf of countless causes reveal her lung power. She's a notorious scrapper, too, running through a half-dozen orchestral scores before finding the version she likes; wearing many hats on the set of a movie (producer, director, actor); and generally running the show the way *she* likes, thank you very much. Barbra's colleague Zsa Zsa Gabor also has a short fuse: She recently went to jail for punching out a reporter.

In life, you find a Kira prototype in every workplace. She's the brilliant but demanding boss whom everyone fears and reveres, who knows the ropes better than everyone, who doesn't tolerate an iota of laziness or sloppiness, and who goes after competitors with a vengeance. If she takes your side, you rise to the top; if she opposes you, better start checking the want ads. In real life, Leona Helmsley offers a dark example. The multimillionaire hotel magnate—known as the "Queen of Mean"—berated her staff for offenses like serving her limp lettuce in a salad. She ended up doing time as a tax cheat.

Which *Star Trek* character wins the prize as the all-time truest

Warrior, the exemplar of the best Warrior traits? Probably Worf, who lets his code of honor lead him in all matters and so uses his great power only to do the right thing for *the ship*. He usually manages to put his personal feelings aside, doesn't insult or offend others even when his blood boils, but shows true Warrior fierceness to any opponent foolish enough to cross him.

✳

Although the very word *warrior* conjures up images of spears and blood and blazing eyes, Warriors do more than fight. They make great lovers, great friends, and great workers, also.

Warriors in love show the same intensity as they do in battle. Worf scares off his girlfriend K'Ehleyr in "The Emissary" by insisting that they mate for life after one short romp in the sack. He proclaims that honor demands a commitment, and has no qualms about making one. In fact, K'Ehleyr's reticence to tie the knot pains Worf deeply. In typical Warrior fashion, he has no ambivalence: He wants her totally, and right away.

You know that Worf's eye won't wander once wedded. His devotion to the woman he loves is total, eternal, and intense. He'll do anything—anything—to protect his love, as he demonstrates in "Reunion," when he swiftly draws his *bat'telh* (the Klingon sword of honor) and kills the man who murdered K'Ehleyr.

Warriors in love bluntly express how they feel, never playing mind games. With a Warrior, you know where you stand. When Worf gets angry at K'Ehleyr, she complains that he won't even look at her. He responds icily, "I'm quite familiar with your appearance." After they reconcile, he tells her with the same directness that he needs her and isn't complete without her. Sounds like a dream lover, doesn't he? What woman (other than K'Ehleyr) wouldn't swoon for a man so committed, so ardent? Deanna Troi eventually goes for him, and so do a few other space babes along the way. Even K'Ehleyr finally succumbs.

Similarly, in "The Collaborator," Kira stands by her man, Vedek Bareil, even after hearing that he lied, cheated, and acted as a traitor. The evidence against him seems indisputable, but Kira refuses to believe it. She challenges the obvious, questioning every shred of hard evidence until she finally exonerates her man. Throughout even the worst times, Kira's commitment to Bareil never wavers. She's the lover that, like Worf, we all long for.

Famous Warrior love stories abound. In the Bible, the great Warrior Samson sacrificed even his strength to win the love of Delilah. Warriors Bonnie and Clyde took on the world together, sticking like glue until their mutual, bloody demise. Warrior Hillary Clinton constantly slugs it out for Bill, while he seemingly philanders and issues platitudes to the press. Then there was Marc Antony, who enjoyed near-total power over Rome after Julius Caesar's assassination. He summoned Cleopatra, the queen of Egypt, to demand an explanation of her political views. All set to punish her for being a bad girl, he instead lost his heart to her. For a while he tried to play by the script, marrying a nice aristocratic Roman woman and trying to settle down as governor of the eastern portion of the Roman empire. But like a typical Warrior, he couldn't suppress his true feelings. He moved to Egypt and shacked up with Cleo. The folks back home weren't too thrilled by his shenanigans. After losing a key battle and ruining his career, he heard a false rumor that Cleo had killed herself, and he followed suit by falling on his sword.

A story with somewhat less historical documentation but just as much drama is that of Helen, the legendary beautiful woman of Greek mythology. She was carried off against her will to the walled city of Troy by Paris, the son of the Trojan king. Helen's husband did not take kindly to Paris's behavior; after all, Paris had been a guest in their home. To exact revenge and restore his honor, Helen's husband rounded up troops, sailed across the Aegean Sea, and for nine long, bloody years laid siege to Troy. That's why, today, we remember Helen for having the face that launched a thousand ships.

If you've cruised the singles scene lately, a date with a Warrior sounds like nirvana realized. Any unmated person will tell you:

The world does not exactly overflow with decent mates who will kill for their love and who crave commitment, too. But is this portrait of the Warrior too good to be true? What happens if your fire-breathing Warrior gets angry at *you?* Warriors worship the one they love, but if you refuse a Warrior's affections, it's shields up, and fire photon torpedoes. If you continue to resist, the Warrior will shut you out completely, treating you like a dead person.

Warriors show the same passionate devotion to their work that they show to their lovers. In fact, many Warriors thwarted in love turn to work as a substitute. Warriors usually make good employees: They enjoy challenges, have great stamina, and finish what they start. Their code of honor demands loyalty to their chosen workplace, so they'll willingly work hard and long without complaining. In fact, they expect to sweat a little; if they don't, and if things seem too easy, they tend to get a little agitated. Many Warriors substitute workaholism for the thrill of battle, taking on everything they can and relishing the constant pressure to perform and achieve.

When Warriors rise to positions of power, they become formidable competitors. Look at how often Bill Gates, the head of Microsoft, demolishes his competition. Antitrust lawsuits and failed merger deals don't slow him down much. Instead he picks himself up, dusts himself off, and prepares to release the next new "killer application." Newt Gingrich ran up the congressional electrical bill by keeping sessions going late into the night in his efforts to pass groundbreaking legislation. By definition, about every military coup ever staged—whether in Pakistan, Panama, or Peru—involved a Warrior who made up his mind to run the joint for a while.

What's a Warrior's worst nightmare? Playtime! To a Warrior, leisure equals death. At social gatherings, Warriors count the minutes until they can return to more pressing matters. The last thing a Warrior wants is to exchange pleasantries, preferring to get right to the point. If you invite a Warrior to your shindig, you can be sure he'll be out the door at the first opportunity, unless he finds an engrossing argument en route.

In one of the all-time funniest *Star Trek* scenes, Worf demonstrates his displeasure at frivolity when he joins his son and friends in the mud baths in "Cost of Living." While Alexander happily frolics and Lwaxana croons that every cell in her body is vibrating with pleasure, Worf remains stiff as a board with a dark frown on his face. Finally, he growls out: "Are we supposed to just *sit* here?"

Warriors shine brightest in times of trouble. They hold their ground when other mortals run for cover, often turning misfortune to their own advantage. "There are times when things seem so bad that you've got to grab your fate by the shoulders and shake it," says Warrior Lee Iacocca in his autobiography. That's exactly what *he* did in his darkest hour, after getting axed from his job at Ford Motor Company at age fifty-six. He quickly got even by snagging the top post at Chrysler and outselling Ford by a huge margin. Plus, he wrote a tell-all book about Ford that jumped to number one on the bestseller list. Less substantial folks would have succumbed to despair, but Lee took a lesson from the beating like a true Warrior, and went on to become an American hero.

Warriors prove their mettle not only in their dynamic actions, but also in their strength of spirit: True Warriors triumph in trials of the soul as well as on the battlefield. It takes unimaginable strength to sacrifice your own needs—and even your own reputation—for the sake of a cause you believe in. Witness how Worf accepts unjust excommunication and allows himself to be ostracized from the Klingon community in order to save the Empire in the episode "Sins of the Father." Few mortals have the guts to incur public disgrace and to assume blame that belongs to someone else as Worf does, even for a higher purpose. The biggest enemy we humans face is the ego; only the greatest Warriors defeat this foe. Worf stands as a model of something we rarely

see on Earth: a person with a heart so brave and powerful that he
slays his own ego—the ultimate Warrior attainment.

QUICK WARRIOR PROFILE

A WARRIOR'S FAVORITE MOVIES:
*Rocky; The Karate Kid; Dirty Harry; Norma Rae; The Termina-
tor; Braveheart; Chariots of Fire;* any Bruce Lee movie

A WARRIOR'S FAVORITE BOOKS:
Shogun, by James Clavell; *Guerrilla Marketing Tactics; Steal
This Book,* by Abbie Hoffman; *Trinity,* by Leon Uris; *The Winds
of War,* by Herman Wouk; anything by Tom Clancy

A WARRIOR'S IDEA OF A GREAT VACATION:
Visit West Point; enter the Iron-Man Triathlon; go on an Outward
Bound adventure; go rope climbing

A WARRIOR'S MOTTO:
"No guts, no glory."

GOOD JOBS FOR WARRIORS:
Sales rep; trial lawyer; police officer; collection agent; football
coach; professional athlete; soldier; union organizer; investigative reporter

WHAT YOU'LL FIND IN A WARRIOR'S OFFICE:
Sales or sports awards; motivational sayings; pictures of air-
planes or wild animals or people doing sports; exercise equipment

A WARRIOR'S WORST NIGHTMARES:
Getting sick; people wearing "have a nice day" buttons; Muzak;
getting caught crying at a movie

FAMOUS WARRIORS:
General MacArthur; Joan of Arc; Rosa Parks; Newt Gingrich; Zsa
Zsa Gabor; Ralph Nader; Bonnie and Clyde; Hillary Clinton; Lee
Iacocca; Susan B. Anthony; Malcolm X; Leona Helmsley; Bart
Simpson; Murphy Brown; Attila the Hun

5

A LITTLE WORF KEEPS THE

BULLIES AWAY (BUT TOO MUCH

LANDS YOU IN PRISON)

*Not to give up under any circumstances should be the motto of
our life. "I shall try again and again, and I am bound to succeed.
There will be obstacles, but I have to defy the obstacles."*
— Sri Chinmoy

When the world gets ugly and people turn mean, most
of us fantasize about responding like Warriors.
Who hasn't longed to tell the boss to shove it, the
cop to drop dead, the IRS agent to take a hike? What kid hasn't
dreamed about punching out the neighborhood bully? But while
we daydream about showing our muscle, many of us slink
through life like first-class wimps. We fear that standing up and
speaking out carries *too* high a price tag; that if we express ourselves with *too* much conviction, people will think we're trou-
blemakers, loudmouths. And so, we deny our Warrior in order to
fit in and keep our names off of the proverbial blacklist.

History offers no consolation: So many outspoken people who
dared to express unpopular viewpoints suffered—even died—

for doing so. People like Stephen Biko, the South African black nationalist who urged his countrymen to stand up against apartheid, and whose reward for challenging the establishment was arrest and imprisonment. After a brutal beating by the police, he lapsed into a coma and died. People like Mary Dyer, a Quaker arrested in the 1650s under a Massachusetts state law forbidding the practice of the Quaker religion. Banished from the state, she nonetheless returned twice to protest the treatment of her fellow Quakers. Sentenced to death both times, she managed to get a reprieve from the governor once, but ultimately was hanged in 1660. People like Salman Rushdie, forced out of his country and still in hiding for daring to write *The Satanic Verses*. And people like the many young students killed in Red China a few years ago for protesting government policies.

No wonder our mantra becomes "Don't make waves. This will pass." It certainly seems that the nail that sticks up gets pounded down. Ironically, though, the cowards' path may demand an even higher toll than the way of the Warrior. Each time we get treated like dogs and don't bark, each time we see injustice around us and look the other way, we experience a bit more anger at ourselves, a bit more despair, a bit more fear of ever taking a risk. That's what Shakespeare meant when he wrote, "Cowards die many times before their deaths; the valiant never taste of death but once."

In the classic episode "Plato's Stepchildren," a dwarf named Alexander lets himself get used and abused by people called Platonians, who happen to have supernatural powers that he lacks. Like a total dweeb, Alexander does everything his tormenters command him to do. Filled with self-pity and lacking self-esteem, he assumes that he's quite inferior to the Platonians and becomes paralyzed into inaction. Meanwhile, the Platonians strut their stuff shamelessly, boasting about their invincibility—until Kirk comes along. When Alexander sees Kirk defy the Platonians even at risk of death, he finally becomes inspired to stand up for himself, summoning his own courage and power.

Like Alexander, we let bullies exploit us all too often, even believing we deserve the mistreatment if it goes on long enough. Anything to avoid a volatile confrontation: We sit back and let people act like jerks, thinking passivity the better, more socially acceptable option. But as "Plato's Stepchildren" shows, the low-profile, "kick-me" strategy often merely strengthens the enemy's resolve and undermines our own.

"Avoiding danger is no safer in the long run than outright exposure. The fearful are caught as often as the bold," said Helen Keller. To paraphrase, playing it safe leads to grief as often as making a fuss, plus it gives you much less satisfaction. In fact, for every famous person who suffered for taking an aggressive stand, we can find another one undone by fear and passivity.

Edward II of England, for instance—a reluctant king if ever there was one—brought about his own downfall by playing dead. Fourth in line for the throne, he had no expectation that he'd ever inherit the crown, and certainly no interest in it, either. But after all three of his brothers suddenly died, Edward—lazy, self-indulgent, and distracted—got the job. He wasn't exactly qualified or enthusiastic. Running an army? Not his cup of tea, thanks. Ruling a country? Please, let someone else handle it. And so, while Edward partied on, the infuriated nobles seized control of Parliament. They also kidnapped and killed Edward's favorite courtier, a pretty effective way of keeping him from meddling in affairs of state. Ultimately, his own wife raised an army and imprisoned him. Eight months later, he was murdered in his jail cell. And so Edward's hands-off, passive strategy led to his final demise.

Look what happens on *Star Trek* when the main characters go soft. In "Where No Man Has Gone Before," Kirk stands idly by as his old friend Gary Mitchell gains supernatural powers and becomes dangerous. Sure, Kirk's loyalty to his friend is touching, but it nearly gets him killed when Mitchell violently turns against him. Kirk finally (and sadly) realizes that he must either kill Mitchell, or get killed himself. Similarly, in "Datalore," Data lets his pathological brother, Lore, bully him around. Lore shows his thanks by áttempting to switch Data off. In the end, Data survives only by beaming Lore out into space.

How many times in your own life have you lived to regret acting like a peacenik instead of like a Warrior? You say nothing when your boss mistreats you because you want to keep your job, and then you get fired anyway. You pay the outrageous repair bill without protest, then your engine blows up. You let your spouse "get away with murder" to preserve the peace; then she runs off with someone else.

Does this mean you should fire photon torpedoes at the next hint of a slur? Should you draw your sword the next time someone makes a coarse remark about your ancestors? Of course not. You must choose your battles carefully, but not so carefully that you *never* get tough. If you flee instead of fight too many times, your inner Warrior will either atrophy and die, or it will explode, turning savage. Every meek and mild person has a breaking point, a point where Dr. Jekyll turns into Mr. Hyde. Anger repressed too long inevitably erupts in shocking ways, sometimes turned against others, sometimes against the self—as in suicide.

"All cruelty springs from weakness," said the Native American leader Seneca; in the *Next Generation* episode "The Survivors," pacifist Kevin Uxbridge provides a case in point, sitting back and doing nothing as invading Husnocks attack his planet. He won't even defend his own home, until his beloved wife gets killed. Then Kevin has a fit, transforming from mild-mannered peace lover to terminator. He uses his superpowers to kill the entire Husnock race—fifty billion people—in a flash.

Every day in the daily news you hear about some meek person who suddenly flips out: the "quiet, polite" neighbor who kills his entire family; the "soft-spoken, private" gentleman who goes berserk with an automatic. Stories like these are all too familiar. Recently, during finals week at Harvard, for instance, a pre-med student stabbed her roommate forty-five times before barricading herself in the bathroom and committing suicide. Why? The roomie wasn't quiet enough to suit her. Or remember back in 1991, when a man killed twenty-three people eating lunch at a cafeteria in Texas. Why? Because he had a grudge against women.

Of course, these are extreme examples. Repression rarely leads to mass murder, thank goodness, but it does often cause *some* type of trouble. We turn the other cheek today; tomorrow we get an ulcer. We put up with grief this week, next week we fly into a rage—at the wrong time, maybe even at the wrong person. Then we feel guilty, ashamed.

Imagine how different we would feel if we calmly but forcefully spoke our minds to the "perpetrators" at the outset, making no excuses, showing no fear. The greatest Warriors never let rage build up, and this is the secret of their power. Encountering injustice, they react immediately. They let principle guide them—not anger—and so they radiate strength, not hysteria.

In the *Next Generation* episode "Redemption," Worf asks the Klingon ruler, Gowron, to revoke his excommunication from the Klingon community and set the record straight. While making his request, Worf stands tall, speaks loudly, and acts as if he fully expects Gowron to consent. When Gowron refuses, Worf doesn't rant. Instead, he calmly plots his next move, positioning himself strategically so that Gowron can't refuse him in the future. Worf radiates great strength and power because he acknowledges his own emotions, and yet controls them. He hides nothing, represses nothing. He doesn't store up volcano anger that he fears letting loose; he has no secret weaknesses that he dreads exposing. No enemy can exploit Worf's hidden vulnerabilities—he confronts them himself, and so has nothing to fear from another.

Back on Earth, many cultures systematically train Warriors through rituals that force them to conquer fears and other inner problems, as Worf has done. Some Native American tribes, for instance, send their young people on a "vision quest." After receiving guidance from a holy man, "questers" venture into the wilderness alone and remain there for days, praying and seeking divine guidance. You can bet that after several days on their own in the woods, any lurking fears they have come to the surface. But if they stick it out and conquer their own terror, they may get a divine vision, and that's the goal. The vision quest experience transforms people so much that they often receive a new name afterward to symbolize what they've undergone.

The same idea—that to become outwardly formidable one needs to conquer the inner problems first—is central to the martial arts. To succeed in any martial art, you must develop your self-confidence and your concentration. Certainly you need to learn the necessary moves—kicks, chops, throws—but ultimately Aikido, Tae Kwon Do, and the other martial arts help students to discover weaknesses in their psyches and reveal ways to become inwardly stronger.

In his words and in his actions, Worf reflects the teachings of the vision quest and of martial arts, showing us that a Warrior's true strength lies not in muscle power but in self-mastery. To vanquish one's enemies takes gumption, but the hero-Warrior takes on an even greater challenge—conquering the "inner enemies": fear, lethargy, despair, hopelessness, envy, and so on.

Too many of us believe we can't change or overcome our problems. "I can't help throwing tantrums," we say; "I was born with a bad temper." Or, "I can't possibly undertake such a big project. I guess I'm just a naturally lazy person." Even after years of seeing therapists and reading self-help books, we can't lose our problems. Why? Because we repress our problems, or try to analyze them until light dawns, and unfortunately, these methods take forever and often don't work at all. But by deliberately harnessing the vast power of the Warrior lying dormant inside of us, we can conquer all the obstacles that bind us, both within and without.

In the *Next Generation* episode "Realm of Fear," the fainthearted Barclay lets his terror of transporting get totally out of hand. He refuses to beam off the *Enterprise*, burdening the crew, risking demotion. His paranoia gets increasingly out of control, until he finally calls forth his inner Warrior and goes for a transporter trip on his own. To his great surprise, he overcomes his phobia, gains self-respect in the bargain, and keeps his job.

Few brave and successful people on earth were born bold: Like Barclay (and like us), they had to overcome fear and self-doubt before achieving their triumphs. Barbra Streisand, for instance, has such gripping stagefright that she refused to perform in public for years on end. Yet she sure manages to muster her courage and put on a great show whenever she decides to do so. Similarly, Olympic diver Greg Louganis had to overcome severe self-esteem problems. As a boy, he endured being called "nigger" (his biological father was from Samoa) and "retard" (he was dyslexic and he stuttered). Even worse, his own adoptive father called him "sissy" because he took dancing lessons. Soon, though, Louganis discovered his gift for diving, and he developed that skill to the highest degree.

Louganis faced his ultimate test during the 1988 Olympics in Seoul, when fate dealt him a blow: His head struck the board during a qualifying dive off the ten-meter platform. He suffered embarrassment, fear, shock, anguish that his career might be over. Yet he rallied his courage; not only did he complete the competition, he won two gold medals. His story doesn't end there, however. As a young man, Louganis discovered his homosexuality, and by the time of the Seoul Olympics, he knew he had tested positive for HIV, the virus that causes AIDS. For six years after his Olympics triumph, he carried his devastating secret inside him. Once again, though, Louganis mustered his courage. He took a role as a gay man in an off-Broadway show and then decided to write his autobiography and tell his story. Today, no longer burdened by secret shame, he is an outspoken advocate of human rights.

If you still fear that invoking your inner Warrior may not be worth it because you may alienate people, consider this: Most Warriors have no dearth of admirers. In fact, a glut of cultural heroes are Warriors, from Bart Simpson to Batman, Bob Dylan to Marshal Dillon, George Foreman to Murphy Brown. We glorify

Warriors, at least in the abstract. Who do we love in the movies? Luke Skywalker and Han Solo; Rambo; the Karate Kid; Dirty Harry; Rocky; the Terminator; Jo in *Little Women*; Katharine Hepburn in anything.

In real life too, Warriors win admiration and respect. Though people may tremble when the Warrior turns on them, they still cheer the Warrior's courage, integrity, and fortitude. "I don't know the key to success, but the key to failure is trying to please everybody," says actor Bill Cosby. When you submerge your convictions and swallow your objections to please others, you end up pleasing nobody, not even yourself.

Warriors serve their friends well, not only by defending them against life's bad guys and providing an exemplary model of courage, but in keeping them honest. If you have a fatal flaw, you can count on the Warrior to point it out. True, it may not thrill you when your so-called pal blurts out the no-frills truth about you, but the Warrior's honesty gives you the opportunity to learn about yourself and to make changes that will ultimately empower you. So forget your fear of losing friends. If you let your Warrior come to the fore, you may find that your friends get inspiration from you.

So now you know you must wake up your inner Warrior to live life with gusto and integrity. But what about the other side of the coin? Can you manifest *too much* Warrior?

Unfortunately, yes. You can't let your Warrior rage wildly, without restraint. Although a little bit of Worf keeps the bullies away, too much lands you in prison—or worse.

Becoming a Warrior means overcoming fear and expressing yourself in a straightforward way; not turning from a withering Clark Kent into a rampaging Lex Luthor. Fortunately, most of us have only an occasional temper tantrum, a mean day here and there. Warriors who go completely over the edge are a rare breed, because most of us have such deep inhibitions against showing aggression that we keep our Warrior under control.

But the pent-up Warrior often misbehaves. It needs to express its dynamic energy one way or another, and so it provokes fits of fury that seem to come out of the blue. Or, more commonly (finding no other outlet), it subverts and turns against the self. Someone upsets you and you end up beating on yourself. You become ruthlessly self-critical and punish yourself harshly for minor offenses. You may even become self-destructive.

B'Elanna Torres usually lets her Warrior rampage freely, but in "Parallax," when she learns she may get a big promotion, she tries to reign herself in and act like an exemplary officer. The "good girl" strategy doesn't work, though; B'Elanna's giant Warrior can't be contained. B'Elanna turns against herself, convincing herself that she doesn't deserve the job, obsessing about her poor record at the Academy, and even withdrawing from consideration. Worf also rages against himself when he doesn't measure up to his own high standards. When he loses use of his legs in the episode "Ethics," he seriously considers suicide because he doesn't want to face life as a less-than-perfect specimen. Worf cuts himself no slack.

Like B'Elanna and Worf, most of us harm ourselves more than anyone else when our Warrior has a snit. Either we beat up on ourselves and make ourselves feel like grade F dirt, or else we act out inappropriately, alienating friends and causing ourselves embarrassment. At least most of us don't cause any earth-destroying, permanent damage because our conscience, restraint, and compassion balance out our rage. However, there *are* Warriors who operate on an entirely different scale: those who cross the line from small-time agitators to big-time destroyers. In fact, the *Star Trek* universe has an abundance of Warriors gone completely off the deep end: Cardassians, Romulans, pre-Federation Klingons, Ekotians, Borg all clamor to conquer the galaxy. They won't join the Federation, they sneak ships into the Neutral Zone, they plot the takeover of Starfleet. And what problems they create! No wonder Picard has lost all his hair. What drives these Warriors to act like the bad kids in a kindergarten class who want all the toys for themselves, making trouble for the kids who cooperate nicely?

Often, it's thirst for revenge. The *Next Generation* episode "Chain of Command" provides a good example, when Picard suffers merciless torture by a Cardassian inquisitor. It turns out that the Cardassian has a major gripe left over from childhood, when older kids kicked him around and abused him; he tries to take it out on Picard.

In real life, we see the sad effects of revenge all around us. A member of Gang A gets killed; his comrades take revenge by killing a rival from Gang B; Gang B, its supremacy threatened, kills two more from Gang A, and so on. You can substitute *tribe* or *family* or *ethnic group* or *religious extremist faction* or *political wing* for the word *gang*. The same story repeats far too often, in too many contexts.

The desire for power is often the thing that really pushes Warriors over the edge. The classic episode "Mirror, Mirror," provides a great example of what can happen when Warriors start dreaming about becoming Leaders. Kirk accidently beams into a horrid parallel universe. In this bizarre world, brutality reigns and crew members win promotions and rise to power by assassinating their superiors. When Kirk refuses to destroy an inhabited planet that happens to lie inconveniently in his ship's path, he finds his own life in danger. To his power-mad crewmembers, nothing matters except conquest, even if it means destroying a planet and wasting millions of lives.

Although the behavior portrayed in this episode may seem extreme, the power-mad hunger for conquest has created havoc throughout Earth's history. Back in the 1400s, Ferdinand V of Spain financed Columbus's voyages to the New World *not* because he was curious about what lay over the horizon but because he wanted to expand the territory under his thumb. Nearer his own shores, he drove out the Moors and ruthlessly curbed the power of the nobles so that he could rule the various neighboring regions of Spain, France, Italy, and Northern Africa.

To ensure that everybody shared the same Catholic views, he established a religious thought-police called the Holy Brotherhood, sentencing those who disagreed with him to a hearing before the Grand Inquisitor. Certain ethnic groups, like Jews, didn't even get a hearing: Ferdinand simply uprooted them and threw them out of the country.

More recently, Manuel Noriega made a giant mess in Panama, torturing and murdering masses so he could control the flow of drug money into the country, and ultimately, into his own hot hands. In Cambodia, Pol Pot, driven to retain his hold on the Communist regime, oversaw the deaths of up to four million people through execution, disease, starvation, and overwork. In Rwanda, Africa, two ethnic groups, the Hutus and the Tutsis, take turns killing each other to win the upper hand; over 500,000 people died there within just a few months.

These incidents show the evil that can result when a Warrior's aggression runs unfettered and combines with a desire to dominate. The picture gets even uglier when you throw in another unsavory ingredient: racism.

In the *Deep Space Nine* episode "Crossover," Kira meets her power-hungry double when she gets sucked through a wormhole into the same parallel universe Kirk discovered in "Mirror, Mirror." In this world, Bajorans and Cardassians consider humans a dirty, inferior race. Kira's counterpart rules the roost, meting out punishment by death to any upstart "terran" who dares smirk in her presence, sentencing all humans to backbreaking labor in the mines. It never occurs to the alternate Kira that Earthlings have intrinsic worth, so her villainy knows no bounds. The same theme plays in "The Best of Both Worlds," where the Borg have no use for humans, and in the classic episode "Patterns of Force," where the Naziesque Ekotians attempt to rid their planet of the entire Zeon race.

These episodes, of course, mirror real events back here on Earth. Fortunately, most racists don't do much more damage than stinking up their own neighborhoods. But if they happen to

possess great charisma, political savvy, or a Warrior's temperament, they can trigger holocausts on a continental, even a global
scale. The Crusades, for instance, began as a religious movement
to recapture the Holy Lands from the Muslims. Soon, though, the
crusaders began to wipe out pagans, heretics, and anyone else
deemed an enemy of the Pope—which generally meant anyone
not white and Christian.

In our own century, genocidal reprisals against Armenians in
Turkey led to the deaths of 200,000 people in and another 800,000
during World War I. And Hitler founded his Third Reich on the
belief that the only people fit to live were those of Aryan descent.

Fortunately, most Warriors who crave power don't have
enough force of character to command armies or wreak mass
destruction. More often, they confine their atrocities to everyday
life, trampling the nice guys in settings both mundane and glamorous. You find aggressive, backstabbing people in factories,
board rooms, school rooms, theater troupes, even in church
groups. Professional dancers sometimes put glass in each other's
shoes to win the best role. Middle managers spread rumors about
their colleagues to keep them from getting promoted. Tonya
Harding tried to cripple her rival, Nancy Kerrigan, to prevent her
from Olympic success. The school bully beats up other kids to
rule the playground.

These malevolent souls suffer at least as much as those they
attack. They may win the prize they fight for, but nobody eats
lunch with them, nobody respects them. How many times on
Star Trek does the aggressor win the battle, only to lose the war?
In "Redemption," the sleazy Duras family finally gets convicted
for treason. In "Crossover," Kira's double ultimately loses control
over her subjects. The Nazi leader in "Patterns of Force" gets
iced. It's the same story in real life: Overdeveloped Warriors
often come to bad endings—as did Julius Caesar (assassinated),
General Custer (killed), John Dillinger (gunned down by federal
agents), Ferdinand Marcos (arrested and exiled), Richard Nixon
(forced to resign in disgrace). So you see, the law of Karma

applies: if you have too much Warrior and not enough compassion or integrity, the hatred you engender in others eventually comes back and strangles you.

Few of us achieve the right balance between self-assertion and self-restraint. Although most of us have too much Mr. Nice Guy and not enough Worf, once we discover how good it feels to talk tough and swagger, we tend to go overboard, blasting every poor soul who breathes in our direction. We forget that the Warrior's heroic power comes from integrity, honor, kindness, and self-control; without these qualities, healthy self-expression turns ugly, even dangerous.

Star Trek repeatedly shows the difference between Warriors who have an abundance of heart—like Worf, Kira, Scotty, O'Brien—and Warriors who have no conscience, no compassion, nothing but a voracious hunger for power. The *Next Generation* episode "The Neutral Zone" provides a beautiful example. The *Enterprise* encounters Romulans in a demilitarized area, where they don't belong. Worf urges Picard to attack the Romulans at once, warning that "Romulans have no honor," and can't be trusted. Worf's gripe with the Romulans isn't their aggressive stance; he respects that. But he also prizes a code of honor above all else, knowing that Warriors who lack integrity—like the Romulans—will stop at nothing.

It's one thing to bare teeth and growl when provoked, but quite another to turn vicious and bite—or even worse, to cruise the streets looking for victims. Because our society sends such conflicting messages about aggression—we decry it in our neighborhoods, but promote it in our movies, in sports, in the business arena—we naturally get confused about what it means to be a Warrior. We think it means overcoming our inhibitions and having no fear about blasting our opponents just because we feel like it. Not so: That's the dark side of the Warrior. The *hero* side of the Warrior, on the other hand, gives us the force we need to achieve goals, to protect the defenseless, and to discover our untapped wells of strength and honor.

If you let your temper fly whenever you get agitated, you don't have the Warrior thing down at all. People with hair-trigger tempers have the same problem as those who can't muster any gumption at all: They fear expressing themselves in a straightforward way, so they sit on their rage until it erupts like a volcano.

A true Warrior has enough courage to speak the truth and do the right thing right away, in all situations. A coward, on the other hand, hides behind heavy artillery. Instead of meeting the opponent eyeball to eyeball and calmly stating what needs to be said, the wimp gains an unfair advantage by bombarding the opponent with out-of-bounds fury.

Suppose, for instance, that your friend offends you by not inviting you to a party. If you haven't developed your Warrior, you'll probably say nothing and get depressed, taking it out on yourself. Or else, you might start sniping: "Well, then, you can't come to *my* party, so there." You may even have a fit at your friend, screaming at her for not caring about you and for all her offenses since 1972. In either case, your friend doesn't get a fair chance to defend herself or even to explain herself. What's the alternative? Act like a balanced Warrior: Let your friend know right off the bat that she hurt your feelings, that you would have liked to come because you enjoy her company, and that next time perhaps you'll make the guest list.

Or imagine that you ask your boss for a raise and get turned down. If you wimp out, you'll say hostile things behind your boss's back, or you'll undermine your boss and sabotage the company by working at a level below your peak capacity. Or you might rant and spew and threaten to quit; maybe you'll even snap a pencil or kick a chair to make sure she gets the point. But if you muster the true Warrior spirit, you'll firmly and immediately tell your boss that you feel disappointed and don't like her decision, but that you want to know what you can do, starting now, to earn the raise.

Both the out-of-control Warrior and the withering wimp have the same problem: lack of courage. But can a quivering coward actually transform himself into a lionhearted Warrior? Certainly! According to several reputable comic books, even Arnold Schwarzenegger was once a ninety-pound weakling; bullies kicked sand in his face. Then he bulked up, woke up his inner Warrior, and became the hulking male-god, terminator-type he is today. If Arnold never developed his inner fangs, he'd still be cowering on the beach, picking grit out of his ice cream cone.

The exercises in the next chapter will help you wake up your inner Warrior and manifest it appropriately.

6

EXERCISES TO DEVELOP

YOUR INNER WORF

It's time to stop feeling like a weenie! No more Mr. Pushover! No more Ms. Yellowbelly! To boldly live as you've never lived before, you've got to develop some chutzpah. You can be braver and stronger, if you practice your Warrior skills. Otherwise, how will you ask your boss for a raise, or return a defective product to the store, or complain to your child's teacher about her treatment o your kid?

If you want to develop muscles, you can't just wish for them. You need to work out, preferably under the guidance of a pro. The exercises on the next pages will help you to build inner muscle so you can assert yourself when you need to. Plus, you'll have the world's best Warrior coach—Worf—to guide you.

(You can supplement these exercises by taking a martial arts course. After all, Worf assiduously practices Mok'bara, a Klingon martial art. How do you think he got so bodacious?)

Use these exercises to become familiar with what it feels like to be a Warrior. As you do the exercises, refer to the Warrior Checklist on the next page. If you practice regularly, the Warrior traits that you experience when you do the exercises will manifest in your daily life.

QUICK WARRIOR CHECKLIST

❑ Maintain direct eye contact as long as possible.
❑ Stand tall.
❑ Feel your power in your belly and let your voice come from there.
❑ Breathe deeply and allow your voice to be strong and confident.
❑ Try not to smile.
❑ Keep your body under control at all times—don't use gestures unless they help you make your point.
❑ Stay focused on what you want.
❑ Don't give up easily.
❑ Keep your language simple and to the point.
❑ Review *Star Trek* episodes featuring Warriors.

EXERCISE 1

Look Like a Warrior

You can do this exercise alone, although it will help if you look at yourself in a mirror. Practice standing like a Warrior and moving like a Warrior. If you have trouble capturing the Warrior look, watch the recommended *Star Trek* episodes to see how Worf does it.

1. Warm up by watching Worf in action. Before you begin, watch some *Star Trek* episodes featuring Worf or other Klingons. Good choices include "Heart of Glory," "Redemption," "The Icarus Factor," "Sins of the Father." Other good choices include any episodes featuring Kira, B'Elanna, Tasha, or Cardassians.

2. Stand tall. Do not hunch your shoulders or allow yourself to slump.

3. Feel your strength. Most Warriors are physically fit. If you have more paunch than power, silently repeat the affirmation "I am strong and fit" until you actually feel it is true. It won't change your body shape, but it will help prepare you mentally for what's to come.

4.   Move with power. Imagine that you have a wire attached to your navel and that someone is pulling you forward. This is how you move from your body's center of gravity, as you would learn to do in any of the martial arts.

5.   Maintain fierce eye contact. You need to demonstrate one-pointed focus and determination. Feel that the only thing that matters is the object or person absorbing your attention. Using the mirror, practice staring yourself in the eyes.

6.   Get serious. Don't smile. Warriors look solemn and are difficult to read. Try to stay poker-faced, showing no sign of emotion.

7.   Control your gestures. Keep hand and body movements to a minimum, using them only when necessary to achieve desired results.

8.   Don't get touchy-feely. Warriors don't like to touch or be touched. Keep your body aloof.

EXERCISE 2

Talk Like a Warrior

This exercise will help you to express yourself with a Warrior's forthright assertiveness. If you tend to mince words and wimp out instead of saying what you really think, you'll find this exercise particularly helpful. Try applying this exercise to different situations:

❏   asking your boss for a raise
❏   asking your teacher for a better grade
❏   asking someone out on a date
❏   telling your friend he made you angry

1. **Warm up by listening to Worf.** Again, before you begin, watch some *Star Trek* videos featuring Worf, Klingons, or any *Star Trek* Warriors. Notice the volume of the characters' speech, the general sound of it, the words they use to express themselves. "Sins of the Father," in which Picard addresses the Klingon High Council, provides a particularly good example. Notice how he alters his speech to communicate with Klingons.

2. **Practice talking loudly.** Warriors tend to have powerful, penetrating voices. When they speak, they sound strong. We don't mean that you should shout; the goal here is to learn how to project. Before speaking, learn to take a deep breath and expel it by forcing it upwards from the diaphragm. Keep your throat open and relaxed. Now do the same thing, this time repeating the line "I am a Warrior!"

3. **Go for the monotone.** Warriors' voices don't have much variation in tone or pitch, except when they want to emphasize a particular point. For instance, when Worf says, "I must protest. I am not a merry man," he puts a huge emphasis on *must* and *not*. Also, when he addresses Picard in tense situations, he emphasizes the word *captain*, then pauses a beat before continuing.

4. **Drop the "um."** Warriors never hesitate or hedge in their speech. They use the fewest words possible to say what they want.

5. **Get to the point.** Use simple language and speak directly. Make clear what you want. Don't ramble or qualify your point before you make it, or say things like "You probably don't want to hear this, but . . . "

6. **Use assertive expressions.** Say "I need . . . " or "I want . . . " or "I expect . . . " instead of "I hope . . . " or "I believe . . . " Just for now, don't worry about whether such bluntness will hurt anyone's feelings. Concentrate on getting what you want.

EXERCISE 3

Put Warrior-Talk into Practice

In the following exercise, you'll convert wimpy statements into strong Warrior words. Then you'll practice delivering your Warrior speech in a difficult confrontation.

The Scenario: You are returning your television set to the Acme TV Repair Company for the third time—and for the same problem. You enter the store and a technician greets you.

Your Cowardly Tirade: You approach the technician and deliver this little speech. Read it aloud, paying careful attention to how you feel as you do so.

> Hello. My name is _____. I'm, uh, sorry to bother you with this again, but darn it, this TV still seems to be having a few minor problems. I think the picture is kinda fuzzy—just like it was the last two times I brought it in. I know that it's hard to fix things completely the first time around, but I'm sure you can fix it this time. So, uh, how long do you think you'll need to fix it? Three weeks? Oh, uh, great! My kids can wait three weeks before they get to see their favorite shows again, and I guess if I don't get to watch the World Series, well, I might be able to catch up on my reading! Uh, thanks a lot for your time and assistance. See you in three weeks.

1. Convert the speech into the words of a Warrior. Now rewrite the entire speech in the space below, making strong, assertive statements.

_____

_____

_____

_____

_____

2. **Get inspired.** If you have trouble making your speech strong and assertive, refer to the example below for inspiration.

> Hello, I'm _____. I'm bringing my television back here the third time for the same problem! The picture is still just as fuzzy as it was the first time I brought it in. I expect you to fix it correctly this time. How long will it take to repair? Three weeks? That's not acceptable. I need it in two days, and I want a loaner TV in the meantime. If you can't agree to that, I need to speak to the manager.

3. **Deliver your Warrior's speech.** Stand in front of a mirror and deliver your revised speech to the technician. Look like a Warrior, sound like a Warrior, feel like a Warrior.

4. **Be prepared for contingencies.** Rehearse how you would reply if the technician said the following things:

■ "I'm the manager."
■ "He's away on vacation."
■ "We don't give out loaners."

EXERCISE 4

Identify Warriors in Your Life

1. **List five people you know who have strong Warrior characteristics.**

_____

_____

_____

_____

_____

2. Think about an incident you observed when a friend of yours acted like a Warrior. Perhaps you watched her take something back to a department store without a receipt, or you saw her challenge the umpire's call during a league softball game. Write down details about the Warrior behaviors your friend exhibited, including how she looked, talked, and acted.

_____

_____

_____

_____

3. Recall an incident in which your parents or siblings acted like Warriors. Describe the incident, and record details about how your family member looked, sounded, and acted.

_____

_____

_____

_____

_____

4. **Recall an incident in which your boss, roommate, or someone you work with or go to school with acted like a Warrior.** Again, record details about the incident and about the person's appearance, voice, and actions.

_____

_____

_____

_____

_____

EXERCISE 5

Reverse a Cowardly Action from Your Past

1. **Remember a time in the past when you didn't assert yourself.** Choose an incident in which you wanted to be forceful, but didn't have the guts—preferably an incident in which you regretted your cowardly behavior. Describe the incident, including details about how you looked, spoke, and acted.

_____

_____

_____

_____

_____

2. **What *should* you have said that you failed to say?**

_____

_____

_____

_____

3.   How would Worf handle that same situation?

_____

_____

_____

_____

4.   Reenact the situation, this time acting like a Warrior. Warm up by reviewing Exercises 1–3, above. You can also use the Checklist on page 76 to warm up. The first time you do this, practice alone. Later, you can role-play with another person. When you feel comfortable asserting yourself in this situation, repeat the exercise using another situation in which you didn't summon your Warrior.

Role-play Exercises

This section contains exercises to help you practice your Warrior skills in typical everyday situations. You can practice these alone, but you'll get even better results if you do them with a partner. Once you feel comfortable with these exercises, you can apply the behaviors you've mastered in your real life.

EXERCISE 6

The Boss from Beyond

The Situation: Your boss has asked you to work long hours to finish a project that was poorly planned and given to you late. She expects you to complete the project without complaint. The long work days interfere with other important activities, including the time you spend with your family.

Your Task: Express your willingness to pitch in and work hard in a crunch, but firmly state that you can't work the hours she wants you to because you have outside interests. Remind your boss that this particular project was poorly planned, and that you had nothing to do with the planning. Suggest strategizing together about how to complete the work. Ask your boss to clearly define her needs so you can offer viable alternatives: hours when you can work, hiring temporary workers, and so on.

Suggested Episodes to Watch in Preparation:

- ❑ "The Gamesters of Triskelion" (classic): Kirk tells the Triskelions what he thinks about their "sport."·
- ❑ "Chain of Command" *(TNG):* Picard stands up to a Cardassian inquisitor.
- ❑ "Paradise" *(DS9):* Sisko confronts the leader of a shipwrecked colony, Alixus, and ends up in solitary confinement.
- ❑ "A Matter of Honor"·*(TNG):* Riker joins a Klingon crew.
- ❑ "The Drumhead" *(TNG):* Picard tries to prevent a witchhunt.

How to Proceed: Review the Warrior Checklist on page 76 before you begin. Find a partner to do this exercise with you. Ask your partner to role-play your boss, getting angry when you decline her request. Practice countering her anger by firmly insisting on coming up with a viable plan of action.

EXERCISE 7

The Turnabout Movie-Goer

The Situation: The guy behind you has not stopped talking since the movie began. What's worse, he keeps kicking your seat. It's difficult to hear the movie, and you're getting so annoyed that you can't enjoy the show at all.

Your Task: Turn to face the noisy person, or better yet, stand up and face him. Tell him you can't hear the movie, and firmly but politely ask him to quiet down. Also ask him to stop kicking your seat.

Suggested Episodes to Watch in Preparation:

- ❑ "Prime Factors" *(Voyager):* Janeway sets limits with Tuvok and gives B'Elanna an ultimatum.
- ❑ "Tapestry" *(TNG):* Picard picks on the wrong aliens and takes a dagger through the heart (a good example of how *not to* confront people).

How to proceed: Review the Warrior Checklist on page 76. If possible, role-play this exercise with a friend. Ask him to make noise even after your confrontation. Again, turn around, this time telling the person that you would like him to move to another seat. Muster Worf's forcefulness when you do this.

EXERCISE 8

The Billing Snare

The Situation: You recently received your phone bill and noticed charges for calls that you didn't make. This is the second time in three months that this has happened

Your Task: Call the billing department at the telephone company to request an adjustment to your bill. You also need to talk with someone who can help you find out why this keeps happening.

Suggested Episode to Watch in Preparation:

❑ "Move Along Home"*(DS9):* Quark is forced to yield to his customer's demands.

How to Proceed: Role-play calling the phone company and describing the problem. Express your feelings ("I am annoyed that this has happened two times in the last three months"). Say what you want ("I want a billing adjustment and I want to know why this keeps happening"). Ask to speak to supervisors if you meet resistance from the people you speak with, and don't give up until you feel satisfied that the problem is resolved.

Part Three

KNOWING ISN'T EVERYTHING, IT'S THE

ONLY THING: LIFE LESSONS FROM

THE ANALYSTS, SPOCK, DAX,

DATA, Q, ODO, AND TUVOK

7

LOGIC, FACTS, AND A WELL-CONTROLLED

LIBIDO: THE ANALYST'S CREDO

From a drop of water a logician could infer the possibility of an
Atlantic or a Niagara without having seen or heard of one or the
other.

— Sir Arthur Conan Doyle, *A Study in Scarlet*

Spock finds human emotion revolting: His counterpart
Data—like the Tin Man in *The Wizard of Oz*—wants a
feeling heart more than anything in the universe. Yet
both of these characters love facts, feed on logic, and have an
annoying habit of always being right. They both see things as
they are, their vision unclouded by emotion or the illogical need
to be "nice."

In the classic episode "Where No Man Has Gone Before,"
Spock advises Kirk to knock off their mutual friend Gary
Mitchell after Mitchell goes power-mad. Kirk can't bring himself
even to *reject* Mitchell: His love for his old pal blinds him to the
horrible truth. Spock has no such problem. He clearly sees the
danger Mitchell poses, because he relies strictly on logic and
observation. Yet Spock isn't heartless: In fact, he admits that he

"feels" for Mitchell. He simply (and rightly) knows that Mitchell has to be stopped. In the end, Kirk *must* kill Mitchell, as Spock predicted.

The true Analyst, like Spock, remains objective even in the most painful of situations. While others emote and tear their hair out, Analysts take a step back, systematically examine the facts, determine the logical course of behavior, and propose the steps needed to achieve the goal. After a car accident, for example, the Analyst stays calm, assesses the damage, and records the relevant facts. Meanwhile, the Leader orders bystanders to tend to the wounded while yanking out the car phone to call the cops; the Warrior incites a near fist fight with the other driver; and the Relater introduces himself to the other passengers, makes sure nobody got hurt, and emotes about the misfortune of it all.

Analysts don't manifest the bold heroics of the other types: They don't slay dragons, although they may study the dragon's biochemistry and find an ingenious way to put out its fire. They don't sweep away damsels in distress, although they may figure out the best route to the kidnapper's lair, determine the odds of survival, and calculate how much slower the hero's horse will travel while carrying two people, one of whom is a princess too fond of eclairs. Because the Analyst rarely displays swift, decisive moves or a bold, take-charge attitude, some people don't consider them heroic. Yet even though they employ the scientific method instead of wild bravado to do great deeds, Analysts save the day time and again.

Analyst Alan Turing, a British mathematician, sure saved the day for the Allied forces during World War II, when he worked as a cryptographer in the British Foreign Office. At that time, Nazi U-boats were terrorizing the seas by sinking Allied ships carrying supplies vital to the war effort. The Nazi submarines communicated with each other via messages encoded by an ingenious device known as the Enigma Machine. The operator turned the dials to spell out the message. By turning the crank on the machine once, each letter would be substituted by another. For

example, *A* would become *L*. To make the code even more difficult to crack, the operator repeated that step a number of times,
so that *L* would be coded as *Q*, *Q* encoded as *X*, and so on. The
Nazis changed the key to the code on a regular basis; for example, after a few days of first changing A to L, they would then
switch and change A to R. This made the code extremely difficult
to decipher. Turing studied the problem, figured out the system,
and built a machine that worked in reverse. By analyzing the
turning of the cranks, he was able to unlock the various levels of
code and decipher messages. His achievement kept the Allied
forces one step ahead of the Nazis, who couldn't understand
why the British seemed to know their every move in advance.

When action fails, when negotiation fails, when all looks hopeless, Analysts like Turing play their role, finding the one missing
piece of the puzzle that makes victory possible. Others jump to
conclusions, make wrong assumptions, adopt pet theories. Not
Analysts. They comb through the tangled web of facts with a
mental microscope to find the one loose thread that everyone else
overlooked. They never take the obvious at face value, but relentlessly search for the truth, paying painstaking attention to detail.
Next to facts, Analysts love investigation most, and true to form,
leave no stone unturned in their research. Diogenes, who
searched the world with a lamp looking for an honest man, provides a good example. Who but an Analyst would have the
patience to keep up such a challenging search for years and years?

"God is in the details," said Gustave Flaubert; any true Analyst
would agree. Rigorous attention to minutiae sets Analysts apart
from other mortals and gives them their edge. In fact, Sherlock
Holmes—every Analyst's hero—repeatedly demonstrates the
power of attending to the small, the ordinary, the seemingly
insignificant, using his painstaking investigative methods to evaluate "trifles" and catch culprits who elude everyone else.

In "Spectre of the Gun," only Spock's exhaustive analysis res-
cues the crew from a wipeout gunfight. Kirk fails to negotiate a
truce; McCoy deploys a neutralizing agent but it doesn't work.

Meanwhile, Spock examines all the facts step-by-step, asking *why* didn't the neutralizer work; *why* did negotiations fail? He finally deduces that the enemy is not real but merely an illusion. His timely insight opens the door to escape.

Likewise, in "Ex Post Facto," Tuvok rejects "indisputable" evidence proving that Paris killed someone. Though a live recording of the crime recorded on a chip implanted in Paris's brain makes it abundantly clear that Paris did it, Tuvok doesn't buy it. He mind-melds with Paris to access the implanted chip and reviews the action again and again, turning over every stone, considering every remote possibility, until he finally realizes that the angle from which the recording was made indicates that a person shorter than Paris was the killer.

Although primarily a Relater, Abraham Lincoln had some of Tuvok's abilities as a legal Analyst. A famous anecdote reveals his prowess. In 1858, Lincoln, then a prairie lawyer, defended a man named Armstrong, who was accused of killing someone with a slingshot during a drunken brawl. To the townspeople, it seemed an open-and-shut case. An eyewitness named Allen had seen everything. He said there was a full moon overhead that night, and he was only 150 feet away when a fight broke out at eleven o'clock. On cross-examination, Lincoln asked the witness to repeat the story at least a dozen times. Yes, Allen said, he could see Armstrong clearly, because the moon was so bright. Lincoln then picked up an almanac and thumbed to the page that listed meteorological conditions. In black and white, the almanac showed that at 11:00 P.M. on the night of the murder, the moon had fallen so low on the horizon that it was barely visible. The witness, his credibility shot, slunk off the stand. Lincoln then mustered other solid evidence and a verdict of "not guilty."

Analysts make their mark early in life by taking apart their toys to see how they work. In adolescence, they dissect their stereo systems while other kids dance to the music. In adulthood, they hack on their computers all night and go to parties to observe the scene while others actually have a good time. At their best, they make brilliant scientific discoveries, crack insoluble crimes, discover the secrets of the universe.

Did you ever know someone who could solve any riddle or trick question in a flash, who got all the colors in Rubik's Cube to line up while you were still reading the instructions? Analysts can mentally leap beyond the rest of us because their intense curiosity and outstanding reasoning ability lets them consider every possibility, including the possibility that there are possibilities they haven't considered. They examine and analyze facts until they exhaust them, and, still pursuing an answer, may jump even beyond the facts and into the realm of intuition.

Because they have such keen observational powers and such extraordinary ability to synthesize vast amounts of information into a logical whole, Analysts sometimes seem to possess abilities bordering on the mystical. Albert Einstein provides an obvious example. In his work he merely followed the scientific method, examining facts and manipulating data using his amazing powers of analysis and concentration. But at some point, he moved beyond science and into the realm of intuition. One day, while simply "sitting in a chair in the patent office at Bern," he had a profound insight that led to the development of the Theory of Relativity.

Another Analyst who moved beyond the sphere of reason into the arcane was Gottfried Wilhelm Leibniz. By his thirtieth birthday in 1676, Leibniz had mastered the fields of law, politics, diplomacy, mathematics, science, classical literature, philosophy, theology, history, and physics. A very practical man, he also developed the principles of calculus and invented an early type of computer that multiplied, divided, and extracted square roots. But when Leibniz looked up at the heavens, he left science behind. He concluded that pulsating vortexes of spiritual energy make up the universe, and that the universe operates according to a divine plan.

The *Star Trek* Analysts often fathom the obscure more easily than their crewmates do. In "All Good Things . . ." only Data can grasp the possibility that Picard may actually be shifting back and forth in time. The other crewmembers dismiss Picard's claims as a product of his degenerative brain disease and overactive imagination. In "Dramatis Personae," Odo alone recognizes that the schism among crewmembers comes from an alien source.

Spock and his Analyst counterparts chose their professions well. The final frontier gives them a universe of strange phenomena to explore, and they push to do so even when it exposes them to danger. Data risks death to investigate the hidden regions of his own mind in "Birthright, Part I." And how many times does Spock say "Fascinating!" in a blasé tone when danger approaches, intrigued by some aspect of the attacking force? He certainly finds it "fascinating" when Kirk fights a deadly battle with his evil double in "The Enemy Within." Spock remarks, with typical insensitivity, that the threat to Kirk's life provides "an unusual opportunity to study the roles of good and evil in a man."

Like Spock, real life Analysts often pursue information even when it puts them at risk. You might have heard of scientists who actually use themselves as guinea pigs in order to complete their research or to resolve a problem. That's what happens in the movie *Junior*, when Arnold Schwarzenegger, playing a research physician, takes fertility medication to test it out and ends up carrying a baby to term. Although far-fetched, the movie draws on historical precedents—such as that of Werner Forssmann, a German surgeon who developed the technique known as cardiac catheterization. This procedure allows doctors to open a vein and maneuver a catheter directly into the heart. At the time Forssmann was doing his research, no one believed such a procedure would ever be possible. Alone in his lab, Forssmann managed to maneuver the device through his own blood vessel, monitoring its progress on a fluoroscope screen. When he succeeded in inserting the catheter into the right auricle, he knew he needed someone to verify his achievement. So, holding the catheter firmly in place, he went running down the hall of the hospital to find a witness. Nearly thirty years later he was awarded the Nobel Prize for opening up a new pathway for the treatment of heart disease.

Even when they accomplish remarkable things, you rarely read about Analysts in the front page news. Did you ever hear of Werner Forssmann before now? Probably not. Fanfare embarrasses Analysts; they rarely call attention to themselves. In fact, Sigmund Freud—the Analyst's analyst—threw out all his personal notes of decades (twice in his lifetime) to discourage biographers. Likewise, Albert Einstein shunned the spotlight, saying, "I have never lost a sense of distance and a need for solitude—feelings which increase through the years." Such modesty makes it unlikely that we'll ever see a broadcast of the Analyst Academy Awards.

Analysts can drive others nuts with their nitpicking attention to trivia, their maddening precision. For a very funny example, watch Data in "Starship Mine," when he learns to make small talk. While the other crew members desperately avoid their host at a reception because he's a terrible bore, Data animatedly talks nonstop to him about every possible trivial subject. Similarly, in "Conspiracy," Data answers a question about the ship's location with so much detail that the entire crew wants to stuff rags down his throat. In "Errand of Mercy," Spock calculates the odds of survival to the nearest tenth, even while he and Kirk duck phaser fire. And in "Phage," while the crew searches for Neelix's stolen lungs, Tuvok helpfully spews out an infinitesimally detailed list of body parts.

Thomas Edison provides a real-life counterpart to Tuvok. If you ever visit West Orange, New Jersey, drop in on Edison's lab, now preserved as a tourist attraction. The lab houses a combination attic, vault, and junk shop in which Edison collected and categorized every kind of material—from elephant skin to straw—that might ever come in handy in his experiments. His thoroughness led him to win over a thousand patents on devices ranging from telegraph machines and telephones to electric generators, ticker-tape printers for stock market quotations, phonographs, chemical production equipment, and kinetoscopes.

Although most of us can easily forgive Analysts for obsessing over trivia, we have more trouble with their cool demeanor, mistaking it for an icy heart. How many times does McCoy insult Spock for having "no feelings"? In "Court Martial," Spock plays chess with the computer, seemingly indifferent as Kirk gets accused of horrific crimes and must defend himself in a military court. McCoy explodes at Spock's apparent lack of concern, calling him the "most cold-blooded man I know." After Spock thanks McCoy for the compliment, he reveals the method behind his seeming madness. He played chess only to analyze the computer and detect the malfunction that wrongly implicated Kirk. Like most Analysts, poor Spock gets misunderstood more often than any of the other heroic types.

The undemonstrative Analyst rarely engenders public sympathy. Former President Carter, a stoic sort, lost miserably to the affable Reagan, probably more because he failed to enlist popular affection than because of politics. The volatile Di comes out light-years ahead of aloof Charles in the approval polls. Instead of defending themselves when people wrongly accuse them of callousness, Analysts retreat to their labs and get back to work. They don't much care what people think: You rarely find Analysts hiring public relations firms. Look at how long it took Charles to tell his side of the story.

Ironically, it's often the Analyst's complete indifference to public opinion that leads to heroic actions. In "Mirror, Mirror," Spock's evil counterpart in the parallel universe has considerably more integrity than any of his colleagues, because logic alone guides his actions. He belongs to a murderous race, yet he departs from his cultural mores and, after a conversation with Kirk, considers the possibility that killing is wasteful and illogical. (In fact, the alternate Spock's new found pacifism ultimately changes the entire sector, as we learn in the *Deep Space Nine* episode "Crossover.") Likewise, Odo stays aloof from the power struggle aboard *DS9* when everyone else fights in "Dramatis Personae," and Data refuses to join his brother in a grab for power in "Datalore."

Of all the *Star Trek* Analysts, Spock provides the best example of the type. He relies on logic and facts and represses emotions, but doesn't deny that he has them. He occasionally reminds the crew that he is half human, and therefore does feel things, though he favors reason over emotion. Data shares Spock's love of investigation and detail. He also has the requisite detached demeanor, but in his case, it comes from a complete lack of emotion rather than from an ability to control his feelings. Logically, though, he understands that humans have emotions and, like any information-thirsty seeker, he longs to know about emotions—he wants to feel how feelings feel. Tuvok, Odo, and Dax also have many Analyst features, but like Data, their emotions are so submerged that they fall on the extreme end of the scale.

Although Analysts may happily spend their lives hacking through the night, they are quite capable of falling in love. They usually enjoy the experience more than their poor mates, who don't exactly get treated to whirlwind romance. Analysts in love don't sing romantic ballads or swoon when their beloved appears. Emotional displays embarrass them, and so they maintain a "hands-off, I'm thinking" facade. Like Spock, Analysts *do* feel; they simply don't show their feelings to the outside world—or even to their intimates.

The Analyst's hard veneer may occasionally crack, but only under great duress. Spock gets downright amorous a few times, but only under the influence of some irresistible force. In "This Side of Paradise," he "gets spored" and loses his heart, but he has an excuse: The spores made him do it. In "Amok Time," he goes into heat, driven by his out-of-control hormones. He explains that Vulcans only mate when their biology goes bonkers; at other times, they're too repressed. In "All Our Yesterdays," he hurls into a romance in a past time, then blames his fling on the primitive history of his race. Spock feels humiliated when he loses strict emotional control and gets a crush, because whenever his shell gets pried open, his repressed feelings pour out like lava.

The icy Analyst may have fire inside, but only a very perceptive partner knows. If you date someone who keeps you at arm's length, you'll probably assume she doesn't like you and dump her in a flash. To forge a successful relationship with an Analyst, you need great self-confidence so you don't take the cold shoulder personally. You need to sense, rather than feel, the Analyst's passion.

The *Next Generation* episode "Sarek" provides a good example. Sarek keeps his devoted wife at a distance, but when he gets sick and his emotional control breaks down, we learn that he loves her with all his heart and soul. His wife doesn't need to hear the news; she already knows he loves her deeply, though he rarely gives any indication of this fact. She sees beyond Sarek's protective facade to the core of his heart.

Not all Analysts luck out like Sarek. Romantically inclined partners often find the Analyst's lack of warmth tiresome. Go to a convention of engineers and talk to the spouses who accompany them; you'll hear the same complaint over and over. Their mates don't go for mushy love-talk; they prefer long-winded discussions about technical or philosophical matters. They have no interest in real intimacy, preferring an all-night hack session to a romp in the hay.

Data sure lets down his girlfriend, Jenna, in the episode "In Theory." He goes through the motions of courtship, observing his own affair with detached interest, until Jenna discovers that he has no real feeling for her. When the couple mutually decides to break up, Data doesn't even sigh. In fact, he deletes the entire "romance program" from his memory bank.

Similarly, in the *Deep Space Nine* episode "The Forsaken," Lwaxana Troi set her sights on Odo, who doesn't share her interest in love. He coldly tells her he has "no time for romantic interludes." Lwaxana persists in spite of his protests, finally winning his trust when she mothers him through a humiliating experience. She never ekes even an iota of affection from him, but at least his iciness melts a bit.

The thought of the effusive Lwaxana with stone-man Odo elicits a chuckle, but in real life, many such relationships *do* exist. Opposites attract; unemotional Analysts often fall for volatile partners who possess the passion they lack, while emotional types often find the Analyst's stability and trustworthiness attractive. Unfortunately, once the glow of courtship wears off, real trouble begins. The expressive mate suffocates and irritates the Analyst; the Analyst infuriates the more demonstrative mate by remaining emotionally distant. Countless books, movies, and television shows deal with this theme. Playwright Arthur Miller, a self-described cold fish, wrote about his doomed relationship with the passionate Marilyn Monroe in *After the Fall*. The popular movie *Remains of the Day* studies a similar theme, as does the Barbra Streisand-Robert Redford movie *The Way We Were*, and the television show *The Odd Couple*.

The Analyst's detachment may sabotage romantic liaisons, but it can provide real advantages on the job. Analysts get so absorbed in the minutiae of their jobs that they easily remain aloof from office politics. They don't vie for power or compete with colleagues, and they respect the contributions of others, especially anyone who furthers their own research or calculations.

In real life, Analysts often refuse promotions so they can continue to do the technical work that they love. While other people reach too high and end up in jobs that they hate, Analysts rarely do. They usually enjoy busy work, and may astound their colleagues by getting tremendously excited when they resolve an arcane calculation or discover some obscure feature of a computer program. Not long ago the Internet sizzled with news that an English math whiz at Princeton had solved Fermat's Last Theorem, a centuries-old puzzle involving factors. (Don't ask us to explain it; ask Data.) The furor continued to make an Analyst splash when a colleague found holes in the proof a few months later, and then again a year later when the problem was resolved for good. Although the rest of us wouldn't go into orbit over this sort of achievement, to mathematically inclined Analysts, it's equivalent to discovering a new continent.

In combat situations, Analysts remain as cool as ever, observing the action even while they participate in it. Their cool response often saves them from bloodshed. On the other hand, they don't take direct attacks personally, even when they should. Instead, they dismiss anger from others as irrational, look for the logical solution, and stick to the facts.

When Data gets kidnapped in "The Most Toys," his captor marvels at his polite demeanor. Data sees no benefit in throwing a fit, so he simply ignores his kidnapper's demands, frustrating him beyond belief. He also uses his infallible logic to convince one of his captor's assistants to help him escape.

Analysts certainly think it illogical to defend themselves in cases where they know they acted wrongly. After Spock mistakenly thinks he killed Kirk in "Amok Time," he beams back to the *Enterprise* to turn himself in to Starfleet, not even attempting to explain his motives. He could have used the opportunity to further his career, stepping up to assume Kirk's post instead of letting the situation destroy him, but logic told him to do the morally correct thing. Similarly, in "Prime Factors," Tuvok turns himself in to Janeway after disobeying her orders in order to acquire a device that might bring the crew home. When B'Elanna deploys the device, it nearly destroys the ship by causing a warp core breach. B'Elanna confesses, leaving Tuvok free to hide his role in the traitorous incident, but he confesses anyway, fully expecting to get court-martialed.

And so you see, the very thing that may turn people off to Analysts—their cool detachment—also makes them incorruptible. Emotions don't cloud their judgement, and so they rarely do impulsive or deceitful things to gain unfair advantage or hurt others. Emotions may drive the rest of us to lie, cheat, take revenge, get jealous, but Analysts don't suffer such difficulties.

In their constant pursuit for answers, for the truth, Analysts inevitably question themselves. They scrutinize their own motivations, their actions, everything they feel, think, and do. They hold themselves to the same high standard of perfection to which they hold others, noticing every detail of their own inner being which needs improvement.

The Vedic seers told all aspirants, "Know thyself"; complete self-knowledge provides the key that unlocks the secrets of the universe. On the path to enlightenment, Analysts might have a bit of a headstart.

QUICK ANALYST PROFILE

AN ANALYST'S FAVORITE MOVIES:
Rear Window; 2001; My Dinner with André; Flatliners; The Third Man

AN ANALYST'S FAVORITE BOOKS:
Sherlock Holmes mysteries, by Arthur Conan Doyle; *The Power of Myth,* by Joseph Campbell; Microsoft reference manuals; an almanac; Moody's guides; *Critique of Pure Reason,* by Immanuel Kant; the encyclopedia; science fiction in general

AN ANALYST'S IDEA OF A GREAT VACATION:
Uninterrupted hacking; a trip to trace lineage; attend DecWorld or an Apple convention; take behind-the-scenes tours of history museums in major cities

AN ANALYST'S MOTTO:
"Look before you leap."

GOOD JOBS FOR ANALYSTS:
Software engineer; systems analyst; research scientist; accountant; statistician; philosopher; sociologist; paralegal; bookkeeper; book critic; copy editor

WHAT YOU'LL FIND IN AN ANALYST'S OFFICE:
Reference books; calendars in prominent places; a computer with megamemory; electronic gadgets; Rubik's Cube; index cards cross-referencing files; not much hanging on the walls

AN ANALYST'S WORST NIGHTMARES:

Getting chosen to head the United Way drive; computer crashes; getting roped into a blind date

FAMOUS ANALYSTS:

Albert Einstein; Sigmund Freud; Margaret Mead; Thomas Edison; Prince Charles; Jimmy Carter; Carl Sagan; Thomas Hobbes; Sherlock Holmes

8

A LITTLE SPOCK KEEPS YOU

SANE (BUT TOO MUCH MAKES

YOU DEATH AT A PARTY)

f Adam had Spock on his side, he never would have eaten the apple and we'd all be cruising today.

We humans act on impulse power too often, saying more than we should, spending more than we should, acting before thinking, reacting before understanding, eating the entire bag of chips. In a fit of anger, we tell the boss to take a hike, and we get our walking papers. We buy a sports car for too much money; we can barely pay our bills for the next year.

In the *Voyager* episode "Phage," Neelix loses his lungs to an alien and needs artificial life support. Tired of hospital confinement, he rants and raves, demanding release from the machine that keeps him alive. His little fit nearly costs him his life; he goes into shock and the doctor has to sedate him.

Neelix makes a deadly error that an Analyst would never make: He abandons logic and lets his emotions rule. Although his example seems extreme—most of us wouldn't risk death to satisfy a fleeting impulse—we do sabotage ourselves to fulfill our emotional desires. In pursuit of love, we endure relationships with jerks. To release frustration, we tell off our best friends and end up alone; we yell at our kids and make them hate us.

Catharsis has a good name these days."Let it all out," people tell us when we're angry or depressed or frustrated. So we come to believe that to feel okay, we need to spill our guts. Unfortunately, psychological studies show that catharsis usually doesn't work. In fact, crying often makes you feel sadder; yelling makes you feel angrier; giggling makes you feel sillier.

Now there's nothing wrong with emoting—even Spock occasionally admits this—but you must *control* your emotions to stay sane and out of trouble. You need to know when to take a step back from the fray and completely detach yourself. Certainly, when your life depends on staying calm and objective—as Neelix's did—you can't give in to the urge to rant.

The *Star Trek* Analysts show us an alternative to maudlin overindulgence. They stay serene, poised, and always logical while their crewmates suffer from the ups and downs and occasional stupidities brought about by their own emotional storms. The Analysts spare themselves a lot of agony because they avoid making rash decisions. What's more, their unique ability to remain detached and objective in emergencies keeps them out of trouble and gives them the ability to rescue the entire crew time and again.

To Spock, the prototype Analyst, feelings are a giant, undignified waste of time. He watches as his pals aboard the *Enterprise* all nearly buy it at one time or another because they become blinded by love in an emergency, or get angry when they needed to stay calm. No wonder Spock prides himself on his detachment. It keeps him alive, it keeps him from misery, and it sometimes protects the rest of the crew, too.

The lesson Spock offers comes hard to us impetuous humans. Even though we know it's important to balance sentiment with cold logic, we frequently stifle the voice of reason. We read in the paper that smoking causes cancer, we see the warning labels printed on the pack, yet we continue to smoke because it gives us the buzz we crave. We know that if we speed we'll get a ticket, yet we keep pedal to the floor as we cruise down the freeway. We know caffeine rattles our nerves—yet we drink espresso at midnight. Would Spock do any of these things? Never.

Who wants to act logical? After all, that was our parents' job. They spewed out a constant litany: Don't play with that, you'll poke your eye out! Cut out the horseplay, someone's going to get hurt! If you don't stop that, you'll go blind! Naturally, we got in the habit of ignoring these messages. Now, even as adults, we instinctively tune out the voice of reason, still expecting it to tell us to turn down the music, stop having fun, and go to bed already!

Face it: It's more fun to act out than to act grown up and logical, at least in the short run. Nothing works like throwing a fit or wallowing in depression to make us feel like part of the human race. Emotional problems have a comfortable, familiar feel, kind of like favorite old slippers. Even though our problems cause pain, at least they give us something to commiserate about with our friends. And so, we unconsciously perpetuate our self-destructive emotional patterns simply because we don't know how to strike a balance between logic and laughter.

The dilemma resembles the one faced by Odysseus as he tried to navigate the treacherous waters of the Adriatic Sea. Passing through a narrow strait, he had to avoid two dangers: Scylla, a rock-dwelling monster with six heads, each of which had three rows of teeth; and Charybdis, the whirlpool. As boats passed by, Scylla snacked on sailors as if they were hors d'oeuvres. But the other side of the strait wasn't much better, because that's where Charybdis hung out. Three times a day, she would suck up all the waters, along with any vessels that happened to be floating by.

Like Odysseus, we face a desperate challenge: How do we avoid getting caught up in an eddy of emotions without crashing into the rocks of rationality? Spock gives us some clues in "The Enemy Within," when he says, "I have two halves: an alien [logical] half and a human [emotional] half. They're always at war. I survive because my intelligence keeps control."

Although Spock completely controls his emotions, he never denies that they exist. In fact, he makes it his business to know exactly what he feels, though he keeps some distance from his own feelings. Whenever McCoy accuses Spock of having no feelings, Spock takes issue with him, pointing out that he does indeed have human vulnerabilities. He simply chooses to let his intelligence rule.

Before we can successfully control emotions, we must know *exactly* what we're trying to control. We run into big trouble when we don't face our feelings or when we try to squelch them. Why? Simply put, because we can't. Not for long, anyway. When we deny our passions, we become cranky, imbalanced, and dangerous. The healthier approach is to try and do what Spock does: first recognize our feelings, then understand them, then cultivate conscious control over them.

Spock shows that it's possible to remain level-headed and dispassionate and still be a good guy who's fun to pal around with. He keeps his feelings alive enough to retain his kindness, compassion, and sense of humor. Unlike Data, for example, he at least has feelings, and so he comes closest to representing the right mix.

The few times Spock loses control of his passions, he ends up in big trouble. In "The Naked Time," for example, a strange virus strips away his hold on his emotions. His feelings overwhelm him, consume his energy, keep him from making logical decisions. He becomes paralyzed with indecision, unable to move in any direction at all. The story is a cautionary tale that shows how much power we stand to lose when we don't stay detached, and how emotions spinning out of control can drain our life energy.

Look at what happens to people in the news when they lose control over their emotions: Coach Woody Hayes punches out a player on the opposing team and gets fired from Ohio State. Mike Tyson beats up on his wife. Residents of South Central Los Angeles, furious over the verdict in the Rodney King case, erupt into a rampage, burning the neighborhood and killing dozens of people.

A jilted lover in The Bronx gets angry at his girlfriend and sets a fire in a dance club, killing eighty-seven people inside. Jack Nicholson gets so enraged at another driver that he takes out a golf club and swings at the guy's car. A mother in Texas so covets a slot on the cheerleading team for her daughter that she hires hit men to assassinate her daughter's biggest rival.

Of course, these are extreme examples. Most of us keep the lid on our emotions enough to avoid engaging in perverse acts. Even so, emotions have a way of pushing us to do things that we later regret—unless we enlist the help of the inner Analyst. The Analyst helps us to face facts so that we make good decisions without letting emotional pressures get in our way, and so we don't knock our heads (or someone else's head) against walls, or chase after impossible dreams. It also lets us maintain some perspective on life, so that we don't drown in sorrow or fly off the handle when things get tough, or do crazy impulsive things that land us in big trouble.

So many professions require the Analyst's objectivity and good sense. How can doctors make life-and-death decisions without having professional distance, impeccable logic, and a good grip on all the details of the case? If they let their emotions run amuck every time a patient gets sick, they become totally useless. Likewise, teachers need to control their emotions to manage behavior problems in the classroom, or they'll end up in court for assault. Artists and writers must stay aloof when critics slam their work or they'll never produce anything.

In the *Next Generation* episode, "Coming of Age," Wesley's friend Jake flunks his entrance exams to Starfleet Academy. He has zilch perspective on his failure, and so spirals into an emotional frenzy, seizes a shuttlecraft and goes on a Kamikaze flight. His lack of inner Analyst not only sabotages his future in Starfleet, but also nearly gets him killed.

Garak also comes close to ruining his career and ending his life in the *Deep Space Nine* episode "The Wire," when he becomes overwhelmed by guilt. He feels so bad about his past mistakes that he refuses to let Dr. Bashir remove an implanted pain device from him, though it keeps him in constant agony and will soon kill him. If Garak possessed even an iota of Spock's detachment, he'd certainly never let himself suffer to such an extent.

A famous prayer goes: "God grant me the serenity to accept the things I cannot change, the courage to change the things that I can, and the wisdom to know the difference." Jake and Garak might have benefited from the wisdom of this beautiful prayer, which embodies the Analyst's creed. To accept the things you can't change, you need the Analyst's detachment. To change the things you can, you need the Analyst's drive for perfection. To have the wisdom to know the difference, you need the Analyst's clearheaded logic.

You also need the Analyst's attention to detail, though observing minutiae may drive you crazy. If you consider yourself the "big-picture type," if you have no patience for detail-work, you'll eventually get yourself into a mess. Add the numbers wrong, and you bounce checks. Forget an essential ingredient, and the cake tastes like clay. Misspell a word on your résumé, and you don't get hired. Make a mistake in the computer program, and your satellite goes into the wrong orbit.

So many times disaster results from failure to draw on the Analyst's strengths when completing critical operations. The space shuttle *Challenger* exploded because engineers ignored the warnings about the now-notorious "O" rings. Intel lost a fortune by overlooking the flaw in its Pentium chip before releasing it, and the company compounded the error by failing to evaluate and respond to the needs of its customers. The designers of the *Titanic* created sixteen watertight compartments and believed that any encounter with an iceberg could puncture no more than four of them. They were off by one; on its maiden voyage, the unsinkable ship rammed the berg, lost five of the compartments, and went down in less than three hours.

Though Spock and Data and Odo and Tuvok may seem to go overboard in their love of particulars, they often prevent catastrophes by obsessing over trivia. When the rest of the crew gets distracted, the *Star Trek* Analysts plod along, noticing the small details that keep all systems operating.

By now you know that you need a healthy dose of detachment to stay sane and out of trouble, but bear in mind that becoming an Analyst means tempering your emotions, not purging them. As the song goes, "You've gotta have heart." Unfortunately, sometimes Analysts go overboard, becoming so "objective" that they could fry their own mothers in oil to further their research.

Nathan Leopold and Richard Loeb provide a notorious example. During the 1920s, these two Harvard students, considered brilliantly intelligent, shocked the nation when they kidnapped and murdered a twelve-year-old boy named Bobby Franks. Their motive for the crime? They were performing a little experiment: They simply wanted to know—for purely scientific reasons—how it felt to kill someone. Recently an ace computer hacker named Kevin Mitnick committed online mayhem when he broke into a company's files and stole 20,000 customer credit card numbers. Why? Just to see how much trouble he could cause.

Of course, most Analysts don't get that twisted. When they go overboard, they merely become callous in personal relationships, creating living hell for family, friends, and mate. Stories about Analysts who freeze out their loved ones rarely make big news. Although a pernicious and pervasive problem, unloving parents and spouses inflict their punishment quietly, even silently, remaining aloof and inaccessible to the people who need them. They show no patience for the feelings of others, turning their home life into a cold war, leaving a trail of casualties behind them. Their spouses turn to the bottle or swell the enrollment lists at mental health centers. Their children flunk out of school, turn to drugs, run away.

Numerous movies and books deal with the theme of frigid

Analysts dishing out emotional cruelty to their intimates. Mary Tyler Moore ignores her family in *Ordinary People*, driving her teenage son into madness. In *The Doctor*, William Hurt has no compassion for his patients, treating them like laboratory rats until he gets sick himself. In *Reversal of Fortune*, a movie based on a true story, the remote Claus von Bulow takes it one step beyond, allegedly icing his wife by slipping her too much insulin. And of course in the famous Charles Dickens story *A Christmas Carol*, Ebenezer casts a pall everywhere he goes until the holiday spirit finally transforms him.

Analysts gone overboard create suffering for everyone they encounter, including themselves. In the *Next Generation* episode "Half a Life," Lwaxana chooses the wrong person to fall in love with (once again). Her guy, Timicin, belongs to a society where people spare their families the burden of caring for them in old age by committing ritual suicide when they reach age sixty. Timicin plans his death ceremony as he reaches his sixtieth birthday, thinking it the only logical choice—in spite of Lwaxana's protests and his own reluctance. If Timicin had listened to his heart instead of to the demands of protocol, he might have saved not only himself, but his entire planet. He was weeks away from finishing critical research that could have spared his dying world from destruction. Instead, he let himself die, showing that logic taken to the extreme sometimes becomes completely illogical.

Overdeveloped Analysts show up in every walk of life, from schoolroom to boardroom. They often do solitary work, since they have no particular interest in "contact with people," but occasionally their thoroughness gets them promoted to a prominent position from which they inflict misery on all subordinates. As bosses, they demand flawless performance, firing employees who miss work due to illness or family crisis because "efficiency must be maintained." They try to squeeze every drop of blood from their workers by imposing strict hours, limited breaks, and inflexible working conditions. They make great bureaucrats, worshiping the trite, stupid, meaningless regulations that drive other people crazy, and tolerating no deviations from "the book."

As great an inventor as he was, Thomas Edison was no joy to work for. Although he was the boss, he punched the clock every day just like the janitor or a junior chemist. His work record showed that he often put in eighty-hour work weeks; one of his time cards records 110 hours in seven days. His office had three pictures of Henry Ford—but not one of his own wife and kids. Although he lived in a house near his lab for many years, he never even bothered to remove the carved monogram of the previous owner from one of the doorways, since he spent more time at the lab than at home.

To find an overdeveloped Analyst, go hang out at your local public bureaucracy. Try to register your car or collect unemployment or apply for a building permit, and you'll probably get greeted by an icy clerk who treats you like dirt, berating you for not bringing the correct form or for filling out the form incorrectly.

Of course, you expect to get aggravated at the unemployment office. It's much more shocking to get such insensitive treatment from members of the helping professions, but it does happen. Callous doctors deliver fatal diagnoses to patients while chewing gum, without a hint of concern. Sadistic teachers publicly humiliate students who make mistakes. Sociologists walk unaffected through camps of starving children, taking notes about demographics. When Analysts go overboard, they become myopic, focusing so narrowly on the details that particularly concern them that they lose sight of the big picture. The doctor cares only about treating the symptoms, not about the whole patient; the clerk cares only about whether a number two pencil was used on the enrollment form, not about the client's needs; the sociologist cares only about statistics, not about the hungry kids.

Even on the bridge of the *Enterprise*, stiff, remote officers occasionally drop in and create misery. In the *Next Generation* episode "Coming of Age," the nerdy and humorless Lieutenant Remmick conducts an investigation. He stands over people as they work, takes issue with the tiniest discrepancies, and probes into absolutely every bit of onboard business. Luckily for him, nobody punches him out, but several crew members sure want to. In the end, he uncovers no real problems, finding performance on the ship so impressive that he actually asks Picard to hire him. Needless to say, nobody wants to work with him.

Spock also gets into trouble with the crew when he relies too heavily on logic and neglects human factors in "Galileo Seven." He assumes command of a shuttlecraft after it crashes into a planet inhabited by big hairy monsters that kill a member of the crew. The others want to bury the dead man, but Spock refuses to take the time, saying they must focus on repairing the ship instead. His logical approach infuriates the crew and gets the ship into deeper and deeper trouble. Ironically, he manages to escape in the end only when desperation forces him to forget logic and act seemingly completely on impulse, jettisoning the fuel supply at the last minute to create a distress beacon.

As these episodes show, even when out-of-bounds Analysts seemingly win by thrusting their logic down the throats of their cohorts, they lose. They engender so much resentment by acting cold and unsupportive to others that they can't rally support when they need it most. Back on Earth, we see this happen repeatedly in many contexts. A manager berates her colleagues for being lazy and irresponsible, then wonders why they all vote against her proposed project. A Little League coach screams at his players to master countless complex plays, and wonders why half of them don't show up for the next team practice.

The most extreme Analysts lack not only a warm, fuzzy disposition, but also all respect for life. In the *Next Generation* episode "The Most Toys," Kivas Fajo kidnaps Data to add to his collection of rare artifacts. Fajo is oblivious to the fact that Data is a sentient being. Later, Fajo yanks out his prized phaser to show it off, wondering aloud if it actually works. To find out, he turns the phaser against his assistant of ten years—with curiosity his only motivation. He won't blast Data to bits because Data provides an interesting addition to his gallery, but his assistant has no such value to him. In the *Next Generation* episode "Where Silence Has Lease," the alien Nagilum goes even one step beyond Fajo. He plans to kill half the *Enterprise* crew to complete his research on how humans react to death. Fortunately, Picard deters him by invoking the ship's autodestruct sequence instead of letting him have his way.

If only such incidents were confined to fiction! Unfortunately, mad scientists who lack both heart and conscience—who don't care who dies as long as their experiments go well—periodically unleash terror on earth. During World War II, Nazi doctor Josef Mengele conducted gruesome experiments on concentration camp victims to test their reaction to pain, suffering, and death. In the 1950s, the U.S. government exposed unsuspecting victims to high doses of radiation to test its effects. In the 1960s, researchers in Tuskeegee, Alabama, allowed black men with syphilis to go without treatment to study how the disease progressed.

Depraved Analysts specialize in "hands-off" destruction, finding ways to effect wide-scale ruin without ever leaving their labs. Creating a deadly formula poses an interesting theoretical challenge to an overboard Analyst, not much different from any other experiment. In Japan, the Aum Shinrikyo cult cooked up massive batches of the deadly nerve gas sarin and released it in Tokyo subway stations. As police unraveled the plot, they discovered that the cult planned to drop lethal chemicals over Japan to kill people by the millions. A decade ago, the Tylenol murderer contaminated hundreds of bottles of the pain reliever by injecting a deadly chemical into unopened bottles of the pills. The so-called Unabomber sends explosive devices through the mail to assassinate people involved in research in the computer industry. And on a less deadly note, technogeeks thrill as they unleash new computer viruses capable of wiping out all the information on hard drives across the globe. The people who commit these acts universally show no regret—they pride themselves on their technical genius and care little about the devastation they wreak.

These incidents raise a valid question: As we depend more and more on computers and technology for everything—from learning to shopping to cruising for dates—are we in danger of becoming a society of overdeveloped Analysts? Can Analyst traits fester if we spend inordinate amounts of time immersed in technology? Evidence does seem to indicate some alarming trends linked to the growing dominance of technology. Kids these days seem happier playing Nintendo than talking with friends. They spend enormous amounts of time in front of computer and video game screens. Some experts claim that when kids spend their time hacking instead of interacting, they become socially withdrawn and immature. Kids aren't the only ones at risk; recently a wife wrote a letter to "Dear Abby" complaining that ever since a computer came into their home, her husband has changed from a trim, active, sociable guy into a fat, rude, jerk who spends every waking hour playing some mindless game and shouting at the kids to leave him alone.

Technology makes massive amounts of information available at the flick of a switch, but it can't teach us how to process that information in any meaningful way or help us to develop our sense of personal values. In other words, technology puts facts at our disposal but doesn't necessarily facilitate critical thinking. Until recently, kids learned to discriminate between right and wrong by taking humanities and social science courses. Exposure to these ideas helped them understand and apply the lessons offered by great philosophers, historians, writers, and theologians. Now, computer courses replace humanities courses in schools everywhere, so kids learn how to resolve technical problems, but not ethical ones. Combine that with the fact that young people spend so much time exposed to violence on TV and in the movies, and it's no wonder that studies show antisocial crime keeps rising among youth, or that kids increasingly view violence in an almost clinical, detached way.

Overexposure to technology brings out the overboard Analyst in adults, too. We can't tear ourselves away from the computer when a friend calls, so we keep hacking right through the conversation, giving only half attention to the caller. We expect instant answers and instant responses to all our questions because our hard drive operates at 120 MHz, our fax reaches Japan in seconds via a 28.8-baud modem, and our letters reach the other coast overnight. We can't tolerate any mistakes at all—our spell-checkers and built-in calculators don't make any. (At least, that's what the makers of the Pentium chip would have us believe.) In other words, as technology spreads, we develop the negative Analyst qualities without necessarily acquiring the positive ones we so desperately need. Like overdeveloped Analysts, we shut out the people we care about. We prefer the more predictable pleasures of watching a video or working on a spreadsheet to the emotional effort involved in spending time with living beings. At the same time, we feel lonely, and so we compensate by doing impulsive, self-defeating things such as drinking too much and spending too much—just the way underdeveloped Analysts do.

Truly balanced hero-Analysts don't fly off into cyberspace as a way of coping with their problems. Instead, they dispassionately examine the facts and conditions of their lives, and then make logical decisions based on their observations. They acknowledge that sentiment plays a role, but they balance emotions against the facts to develop a clear picture of what needs to be done. They forego immediate gratification in favor of longer-term—and ultimately more rewarding—goals. If an Analyst realizes she's spending too much time participating in an America Online chat forum, for instance, she looks for the root cause of her sloth and does something about it. That doesn't mean buying a faster computer or subscribing to a different forum or eating an entire bag of Oreos to distract herself from the problem. Instead it might mean breaking up with the no-goodnik boyfriend who never calls anyway, canceling the AOL membership, and signing up for a course at the local community college where real, live human beings interface with each other in real time.

Yes, even you can learn to act like a well-balanced Analyst, applying common sense and getting your facts straight. Marion Barry claims to have had a conversion from hedonist to a more Analyst-influenced state of being, and it got him reelected (and out of rehab). Willie Nelson had a similar conversion, after losing all his money to drink and gambling in his more self-indulgent days. Then he woke up his inner Analyst, saw he would end in ruin if he didn't change, and made some savvy, logical business decisions that helped him regain his former fortune. If Marion Barry and Willie Nelson can do it, b'gosh, so can you.

The exercises in the next chapter will help you to bring forward your inner Analyst and manifest it appropriately.

9

EXERCISES TO DEVELOP

YOUR INNER SPOCK

et ready to sharpen your wits and make decisions based on logic and reason! No more self-sabotage from your impulsive escapades or emotional outbursts. No more eternal procrastination because you don't know the right thing do. To boldly live as you've never lived before, you've got think before you act. You've got to develop some inner detacl ment. How else will you choose the right job, or keep peace wit your volatile in-laws, or negotiate a fair settlement with your foi mer business partner?

This chapter teaches you Spock's most precious secret: how t(make excellent decisions without getting caught up in emotiona turmoil. You'll learn a step-by-step procedure for thinking thing: through. You'll no longer be the victim of your own sloppy think- ing or your anxiety-driven decision-making style. This chapter will help you to wake up your inner Analyst so you can act with clearheaded reason whenever you need to.

Use the exercises in this chapter to help you become familiar with what it feels like to be an Analyst. As you do the exercises, refer to the Analyst Checklist that follows. If you practice regularly, you'll find that the Analyst traits you experience when you do these exercises will manifest in your daily life.

ANALYST CHECKLIST

- ❏ Watch *Star Trek* Analysts.
- ❏ Limit facial expression.
- ❏ Make intermittent eye contact.
- ❏ Don't gesture.
- ❏ Stiffen your body.
- ❏ Move and speak slowly.
- ❏ Speak softly.
- ❏ Don't be touchy-feely.
- ❏ Use a monotone voice.
- ❏ Don't try to convince; stick to facts.
- ❏ Don't skip over details; take all the time you need.
- ❏ Ask good questions.

EXERCISE 1

Look Like an Analyst

You can practice this exercise alone, although it helps if you look at yourself in a mirror as you do it. If you have trouble capturing the Analyst look, review any of the *Star Trek* episodes recommended below and notice how Spock and his counterparts present themselves.

1. Warm up by watching Spock in action. Before you begin, watch some *Star Trek* episodes featuring Spock. Good choices include the classic episodes "The City on the Edge of Forever," "The Devil in the Dark," "The Changeling," and "Where No Man Has Gone Before." Other good choices include any episodes featuring Data, Tuvok, or Odo.

2.   **Stay poker-faced.** Analysts do not let their emotions show on their faces. Don't frown, squint, smile, show surprise. Practice keeping your facial muscles completely relaxed.

3.   **Look askance.** Make intermittent rather than prolonged eye contact.

4.   **Become a stiff.** Analysts keep their bodies a bit rigid. Try keeping your spine erect. Imagine that a metal pole inside of you keeps you from moving fluidly.

5.   **Don't gesture.** Analysts do not communicate emotions through hand movements.

6.   **Slow down.** Analysts do not rush. Make every movement of yours deliberate.

7.   **Shrink from contact.** Don't touch others or encourage others to touch you.

EXERCISE 2

Talk Like an Analyst

This exercise will help you to express yourself with an Analyst's unemotional clarity. If you tend to spew out whatever comes into your mind, you'll find it particularly useful. Apply this exercise to different situations:

- ❑ calling in sick to work
- ❑ inviting a new friend to dinner
- ❑ confronting a dishonest car mechanic
- ❑ disagreeing with your teacher about an interpretation of a poem

1.   **Warm up by listening to Spock, Data, Tuvok, or Odo.** Before you begin, review episodes featuring any of the *Star Trek* Analysts. Pay careful attention to the volume of their speech, the amount of inflection, the general sound of it, the words they use to express themselves.

2.   Modulate. Analysts have non-threatening voices. Practice keeping the volume moderate, keeping all aggressiveness out of your voice.

3.   Inflect selectively. If your voice rises and falls too much, you'll come across as emotional. Maintain control over your tone and pitch. You might practice talking with no inflection whatsoever, then try inflecting just one word at a time.

4.   Don't persuade. Analysts don't attempt to convert listeners. State the facts without emotional attachment.

5.   Slow down. Give yourself time to present all the relevant data, without rushing. Analysts never hurry, because they might miss an important detail.

6   Just the facts, Ma'am. Analysts avoid expressing subjective opinions. Try to stick to the facts.

7.   Detailed is beautiful. Give accurate facts, with all relevant supporting information. Don't get sloppy and skip over minor points.

8.   Use "processing" expressions. Say, "It is my observation " or "I believe . . ." instead of "I know . . ." or "This is how it is."

9.   Ask good questions. Analysts never miss a chance to gather more information. Take time to prepare your questions. When you don't understand something, ask for clarification. This step is absolutely critical to successful decision-making.

EXERCISE 3

Solving a Difficult Problem in Your Own Life—Analyst Style

In this exercise, you'll use a systematic, logical approach to resolve a difficult problem that you currently face. Answer all questions completely; use extra paper if necessary.

1. **Identify a problem in your life that you want to solve.** To
   find a problem to work on, focus on the different areas of
   your life one by one: work, finances, love, health, family,
   spirituality, friends. As you review each category, ask yourself if something in that aspect of your life makes you feel
   particularly stuck or unhappy. Describe the problem below,
   being as specific, objective, and accurate as possible.

   _____

   _____

   _____

   _____

   _____

2. **How serious is this problem?** What have been the effects on
   your health, psyche, family, and friends? What facts do you
   have to support your conclusions? How many times has the
   problem occured in the last week, month, year? How much
   time did you spend on it? How much did it cost you? How
   will you know if the problem improves? (Use additional
   paper if necessary.)

   _____

   _____

   _____

   _____

   _____

   _____

3. **List the causes of the problem below.** Is there a people issue? Equipment issue? Environmental issue? Materials issue? Financial issue?

Cause #1:

_____

_____

Cause #2:

_____

_____

Cause #3:

_____

_____

Cause #4:

_____

_____

4. **How can you address each of the causes you listed above?**

To correct Cause 1, I can:

_____

_____

_____

To correct Cause 2, I can:

_____

_____

_____

To correct Cause 3, I can:

_____

_____

_____

To correct Cause 4, I can:

_____

_____

_____

5. **Prepare an action plan for implementing each of the corrective actions listed above.** For each corrective action, decide exactly what you will do and when, how, and where you will do it. If other people are involved, anticipate their actions and responses.

6. **Execute your plan.** Think about what steps you can take to prevent the problem from recurring.

EXERCISE 4

Identify Analysts in Your Life

1. List five people you know who have strong Analyst characteristics.

    _____

    _____

    _____

    _____

    _____

2. **Think about an incident you observed when a friend of yours acted like an Analyst.** Perhaps you watched him analyze a difficult problem and come up with a solution that no one else thought of, or saw him stay rational and calm in a difficult confrontation, or noticed him paying great attention to facts that you overlooked. Write down details about the Analyst behaviors your friend exhibited, including how he looked, talked, and portrayed himself.

    _____

    _____

    _____

    _____

    _____

3. **Can you recall an incident in which your parents or siblings acted like Analysts?** Describe the incident, and record details about how your family member looked, sounded, and acted.

_____

_____

_____

_____

_____

_____

4. **Recall an incident in which your boss or one of your co-workers acted like an Analyst.** Again, record details about the incident and about the person's appearance, voice, and actions.

_____

_____

_____

_____

_____

_____

5. Now go back through each of the incidents you wrote about above, and remember how you felt as you observed your friend, your family member, and your boss or colleague act like an Analyst. Were you frightened, proud, intimidated, inspired? Write down the feelings you remember having during and after each incident. This will give you some information about your own readiness to become an Analyst.

Incident #1:_____

_____

_____

Incident #2:_____

_____

_____

Incident #3:_____

_____

_____

EXERCISE 5

Learn from an Impetuous Decision in Your Past

1. Remember a time in the past when you failed to consider all the facts and made a bad decision. Choose an incident that ended up creating real problems for you. Describe the incident, including details about how you looked, spoke, and acted during and after the incident.

_____

_____

_____

_____

_____

_____

2. What *should* you have done that you failed to do?

_____

_____

_____

_____

_____

3. How would an Analyst handle that same situation?

_____

_____

_____

_____

_____

4. **Reenact the situation, this time acting like an Analyst.** Warm up by reviewing Exercises 1–3. You can also use the Analyst Checklist on page 118 to warm up. When you feel comfortable using Analyst traits in this situation, move on to another situation in which you didn't summon your Analyst.

Role-play Exercises

This section contains exercises to help you practice your Analyst skills in typical everyday situations. You can practice these alone, but you'll get even better results if you do them with a partner. Once you feel comfortable with these exercises, you can apply the behaviors you've mastered in your real life.

EXERCISE 6

The Neighbor on the Edge of Fury

The Situation: Your dog broke loose from his run and trampled your neighbor's garden. She's furious, threatening to call the pound.

Your Task: Allay your neighbor's anger by asking what concrete steps you can take to repair the damage done, and by suggesting ways to prevent a recurrence.

Suggested Episodes to Watch in Preparation:

- ❑ "Amok Time" (classic): Spock thinks he kills Kirk, and needs to make amends.
- ❑ "Datalore" *(TNG):* Data attempts to appease his rabid brother.

How to Proceed: Review the Analyst Checklist on page 118 before you begin. Find a partner to do this exercise with you. Ask your partner to role-play an irate neighbor who is furious that her prize-winning garden has been violated. Remain objective and impassive in spite of her threats and insults, sticking to the facts. Ask lots of questions to clarify the extent of the damage your dog caused and what you can do about it. For instance, find out what type of plants your dog completely ruined, if any might be salvageable and how you can revivify them, how much it will cost to re-plant the garden, if she can fence the garden to avoid future mishaps, and so on. Also offer ideas for preventing your dog from escaping in the future. And of course, offer your apologies—but don't ooze. Maintain dispassion throughout.

EXERCISE 7

The Computer Culprit

The Situation: You enter your cubicle at work in the morning and notice that your computer is running. A paper coffee cup with red lipstick stains sits atop the report that you slaved to put together over the past few days. You notice several coffee stains on the cover of the report. You also notice that your disk file has been rifled, and floppies lie scattered over your desk. One is in the disk-drive and there are several on the floor. You know the culprit must be either your colleague P., or your boss, M.

Your Task: Discover who made this mess, and inform that person of your displeasure in order to prevent a recurrence.

Suggested Episodes to Watch in Preparation:

- ❑ "Necessary Evil" *(DS9):* Odo solves a murder mystery.
- ❑ "Ex Post Facto" (*Voyager*): Tuvok conducts an investigation against Paris.
- ❑ "Spectre of the Gun" (classic): Spock figures out the truth about the Melkots.

❏ "Elementary, Dear Data" *(TNG):* Data plays Sherlock Holmes.

❏ "All Good Things . . . " *(TNG):* Picard resolves a cosmic mystery, with help from Data.

How to Proceed: Assess the consequences of confronting each of the suspects before considering the evidence. Then, using your best Analyst skills, study the evidence to discover who, in fact, is responsible. How might Data proceed? Look at the shade of red lipstick and see if it matches the shade worn by either P. or M. Look at the directory of the disk in your disk drive to discover what the culprit may have been looking at. Which suspect would have had more reason to use those files? Consider the personal characteristics of P. and M. Whose personality is more clearly reflected by the situation you discovered? Then, once the evidence clearly identifies a suspect, consider the ends you wish to achieve in the coming confrontation. If the evidence points to your boss, what consequences will result from a confrontation? What approach will allow you to make your point while retaining both your integrity and your job?

EXERCISE 8

The Future Conundrum

The Situation: You already work fifty-plus hours a week, but you just got an offer to take on a lucrative and prestigious consulting job during your off-hours. You don't want to give up this once-in-a-lifetime opportunity, but on the other hand, you already feel incredibly stressed out and have no time for exercise, friends, or fun.

Your Task: List the pros and cons of both accepting the offer and refusing it. Consider all possible scenarios. Gather all the relevant facts, like exactly how much time the consulting position would involve; whether you might get a leave of absence from work; what other consultants say about working for this particular company; what you might gain by *not* taking the assignment; and so on. Work out the financial consequences for each scenario. Try to keep emotions out of the process.

Suggested Episodes to Watch in Preparation:

- ❏ "Journey's End" *(TNG)*: Wesley decides to give up his Adademy training.
- ❏ "Coming of Age" *(TNG)*: Picard gets offered a big promotion.
- ❏ "Mirror, Mirror" (classic): The "alternate" Spock considers his career options.
- ❏ "The Best of Both Worlds" *(TNG)*: Riker is offered command of the *Melbourne*.

How to Proceed: Watch the relevant *Star Trek* episodes, if possible. Also review earlier decision-making exercises in this chapter. If it works better for you, substitute your own difficult decision for the scenario provided. Write out your list of pros and cons, write down alternate options, gather all relevant facts and financial data. When you complete your research, make a decision based completely on the data, keeping your emotions out of the process. If possible, work with a friend who will go through the process with you and ensure that you stick to the facts.

PART FOUR

WHAT'S LOVE GOT TO DO WITH IT?

LIFE LESSONS FROM THE RELATERS,

GUINAN, THE TROIS,

MCCOY, BASHIR, AND KES

10

AN OPEN HEART, A WILLING SHOULDER, AND A SMOOCH BEFORE THE FIRST DATE: THE RELATER'S CREDO

One of the greatest things of living is getting to know people and having them become your friends.

—Mister Rogers

Walt Whitman once commented that he loved to be in crowds of people. He especially liked swarming places like Broadway in New York, where he could feel the pulse of human life all around him. As he wrote in *Song of Myself*, "In the faces of men and women I see God."

Unlike Whitman, most of us don't see God when encountering a teeming mob; we see trouble and search for an alternate route. But true Relaters like Whitman joyfully plunge right in, finding complete satisfaction in blending with "the hurrying and vast amplitude of those never-ending human currents."

Relaters relish human company. The rest of us may need to hole up alone and shut out the world to recharge our batteries, but Relaters get electrified by socializing nonstop. Like pack animals, they avoid isolation above all things, not because they feel insecure when alone, but because they truly get joy out of constant schmoozing. Dinner with friends, parties, family picnics, romantic escapades—these things feed the Relater's soul.

Star Trek's most conspicuous Relater—Lwaxana Troi—relentlessly seeks someone to mate with. She finds most men suitable choices and goes after them with determination, scaring them off with her effusive advances. Does Lwaxana really desire a husband, or does she just want human company in whatever way she can grab it? The truth is, Lwaxana overflows with love for all people, and so doesn't particularly care whom she pursues. She even gives up the idea of marriage when she finds friendship elsewhere, like when she and Alexander become good pals in "Cost of Living," and actually seems to get as much joy from chasing after her prospects as from catching them.

Most Relaters rein in their enthusiasms a bit more than Mrs. Troi does, but all crave opportunities for intimacy—or at least for interaction. Relaters always have something on the social calendar. If nobody invites them over to dinner, if they have no party to attend, they create their own event. And so, the Relater's house often becomes "party central." There's always someone coming over, some bash in the works, some group outing in the wings.

Relaters often become celebrated for their great party-giving skills. While their husbands served in the White House, Martha Washington, Dolly Madison, and Jacqueline Kennedy became famous in their own right for their great skills as hostesses. Martha Stewart made a cottage industry out of peddling advice on everything from how to arrange hors d'oeuvres on a plate to how to escort the last reluctant guest out the door, as did Letitia Baldrige, who was social secretary at the White House during Kennedy's term.

Mingling isn't merely after-work sport for Relaters. Relaters choose in-your-face professions that let them hobnob all day long: sales, public relations, social work, nursing, the theater. On *Star Trek*, Guinan works as a bartender, a job that lets her simultaneously mix drinks and mix with virtually everyone aboard the ship. Troi serves as ship's counselor, communing intimately with crewmates day and night. Doctors Bashir and McCoy spend their days ministering to creatures from across the galaxy. And Kes, who starts out as a cook's assistant, ends up training to be a nurse when her Relater qualities propel her toward a more public position.

Can you imagine Guinan working as a bookkeeping assistant? She would wither and die, yet she shines as a bartender, putting people at ease, anticipating needs before her customers even express them. In the same way, imagine how famous Relaters might fare if miscast in the wrong professions. How about Robin Williams as an engineer, Oprah as an army general, Leo Buscaglia as a bank manager?

Relaters need to find work that accommodates their sociable natures. They suffer terribly when stuck in jobs that isolate them—although they may compensate by socializing with co-workers all day long, organizing office parties, making friends in every department, sneaking in phone calls to their pals, chit-chatting at the copy machine, and gossiping over coffee as long as possible. Their overflowing gregariousness sometimes gets them in trouble; not all supervisors appreciate workers who fraternize instead of keeping their noses to the grindstone. On the other hand, when Relaters can't interact on the job, they become completely depressed and unproductive.

Believe it or not, Abraham Lincoln—who had strong Relater traits—failed in business several times before he found his way to public service. As he put it, "I never did like to work, and I don't deny it. I'd rather read, tell stories, crack jokes, talk, laugh—anything but work." Apparently, the most public of all jobs seemed less like work to Honest Abe than running a business did.

More than a hundred years later, Relater Bill Clinton turned the usually grueling job of campaigning for president into one big party. He took a cross-country business trip with his entire entourage, turning his running mate Al Gore into a travelling buddy. Instead of addressing the American public in the customary political speech style, he held chatty "town meetings," where anyone could ask him anything on national TV—including whether he preferred boxer shorts or briefs—for the price of a hug or very warm handshake. And when his "I'm everybody's pal" style paid off, he celebrated victory by having a gigantic "be-in" on the national mall, playing sax for his electorate. A year and a half later he stood in a parking lot somewhere in the Midwest, commiserating with flood victims who had come to fetch drinking water, telling everyone how much he felt their pain.

Relaters love to shake hands and rub elbows, but that level of contact isn't enough to satisfy them. They need to get up close and personal: No level of intimacy can be too deep. Relaters love to climb inside of your psyche, to immerse themselves in your business; the more they know about you, the better. They have a way of extracting private information from you that you had no intention of sharing, and in return, they don't hesitate to reveal their own deepest feelings. The *Star Trek* empaths—Guinan, Deanna Troi, and Lwaxana—all dive inside of others by using their empathic powers. In real life, skilled psychotherapists do the same thing. So do talented talk show hosts like Phil Donahue, who manages to get the most unlikely people to talk about the most secret things. Barbara Walters is famous for her ability to get normally reserved people like Robert McNamara to cry for the cameras.

Fortunately, Relaters don't have voyeurism in mind when they extract those juicy secrets from you. On the contrary, they genuinely want to help you, want to get deep inside of you to take away your pain. Relaters want to make everyone happy, and in fact, fall in love constantly—with friends, family, co-workers, even with people in the news. You may find yourself spilling your guts to a Relater just because you feel such warmth and acceptance; you know you won't be judged or hurt no matter what you say or do.

Look at how Lwaxana's heart melts when she learns that Odo is the only known surviving member of his species in "The Forsaken." She pursues him with gusto, bombarding him with her considerable affections. When her efforts to love him go nowhere, she finally makes herself completely vulnerable to him, taking off her wig to show how ordinary she looks without it. Even the impervious Odo can't resist her love blasts; he ends up literally melting into her skirt.

Relaters burst with compassion, not just for people but for animals and all living things. James Herriot, the veterinarian turned author from Yorkshire, England, provides a great example. The titles of his most famous books, each a line from a poem by Cecil Frances Alexander, testify to his Relater leanings: *All Things Bright and Beautiful; All Creatures Great and Small; All Things Wise and Wonderful; The Lord God Made Them All.*

Envy the lucky pet owned by a Relater! Relaters treat their pets like royalty. Not long ago an elderly couple in Florida threw a $20,000 shindig aboard a yacht in celebration of their cat's birthday. Relaters attribute human needs and feelings to their animals. Unable to abide cruelty, they sometimes adopt so many strays that their homes look like zoos. Vulnerable creatures in peril bring out the Relater's heroic side, inspiring him to launch a rescue attempt. A few years ago the world watched as volunteers struggled to free a couple of whales trapped in the Alaskan ice; similarly, workers tried every trick in the book to lure a disoriented whale out of San Francisco Bay and into the open sea. You can bet Relaters were behind those efforts.

The *Star Trek* Relaters may seem as different from each other as night and day, but they all share certain qualities: emotional openness, compassion, generosity. The on-board physicians reveal the range of Relater styles. Of course, it's their doctorly duty to "relate" to people. But Bones, Crusher, and Bashir go beyond the demands of the Hippocratic oath. They don't simply care for the crewmembers' bodies, they care for their souls as well. Bones is hardly a touch-feely kind of doc. Quite the opposite; he can be as bristly as a thistle. Crusher, by contrast, is as likely to give you a therapeutic hug as she is to administer an antibiotic injection.

They also lean toward right-brain dominance. Lwaxana Troi and Neelix lean a bit more than the others, sometimes spilling right over into the realm of imprudence. Deanna Troi, on the other hand, could use some lessons in lightening up from her mom, and Bashir gets a bit narcissistic at times. The most balanced Relaters on *Star Trek* are Guinan and Kes. They both let their hearts lead them and yet never get bogged down by the angst of it all.

All the *Star Trek* Relaters embody the quality of empathy. Kes showers affection even on the holographic doctor; Bashir reaches out to the nastiest folks on board; McCoy repeatedly risks his life for unworthy aliens, and Guinan manages to get everyone imaginable to pour out their hearts. In "Ensign Ro," Ro Laren stonewalls the rest of the crew but eventually breaks down and talks to Guinan. Similarly, Wesley Crusher confides to her that he wants to stay aboard the *Enterprise* on the eve of his departure for Starfleet Academy in "The Child." Even the impenetrable Picard spills to her on several occasions; so does Worf.

Guinan and the other *Star Trek* Relaters may seem to good to be true, but they actually have numerous real-life counterparts. Oprah Winfrey offers a famous example, winning the trust of almost everyone she encounters. Her nonjudgmental warmth rockets her to the top of the Neilsen ratings time and again, as she lulls person after person into revealing their messiest secrets. Oprah, like Guinan, really *listens* when people speak to her. In fact, she focuses so intently that she seems to hear even beyond the spoken word. Oprah attributes her success to her vulnerability, which makes her nonthreatening to both viewers and guests. "I allow myself to be vulnerable," she says. "It's not something I consciously do. But I just am." Society rewards her handsomely for her gift; her name constantly appears at or near the top of the list of the country's highest-paid entertainers.

Relaters like Oprah wear their hearts on their sleeves. They shamelessly tell you what they feel, and expect you to do the same. They don't understand or respect stoicism, don't know how to keep a poker face. If you know someone who cries at movies that leave you cold, who even cries at *commercials* when the moon is full, you definitely know a Relater.

Such emotional sensitivity has a flip side. Relaters want everyone to like them—to really, *really* like them—in the same way that they like everybody. Their extreme vulnerability makes them suffer terribly when people treat them with hostility, or even worse, when people ignore them. If they meet someone who doesn't respond to their friendly advances, they go all out to win that person's affection. Often, they waste their efforts and end up feeling despair; they just can't accept the fact that some people will never warm up to them. In fact, much of their gregarious behavior has its roots in a desire to convert everyone on the planet into a friend. This pattern plays out in a particularly wrenching way when Relaters pursue romantic involvements with stodgy, unresponsive Analyst types.

Put all these Relater qualities together—overflowing love, natural trust, compassion for all creatures, unblushing emotional expressiveness—and what do you get? The profile of a typical three-year-old kid. Actually, Relaters have much in common with young children.

We all start life as Relaters, wanting nothing more than to be with family or to play with friends, certainly not caring about political or technical issues. Children naturally trust and accept others, and often have trouble adjusting to the strictures of school; they want to frolic, not sit in rows getting cerebral. Why do kids get so fidgety? Because they naturally resist the way society's institutions—schools and churches and so on—try to suppress their Relater instincts and shift their psychic balance. But resist as they might, in most cases they soon succumb. By second grade or so, they experience the awakening of their analytic intelligence and the pressures exerted by society to "get serious."

Some go too far, completely suppressing or even rejecting their own Relater qualities, but a few manage to stay "forever young," by allowing the Relater to dominate their personality. Like kids, adult Relaters love to play, love to cuddle, love to go to parties. They express their emotions freely, without embarrassment, and don't hesitate to ask the most nosy questions.

In fact, to find an adult Relater quickly, ask three-year-old kids which adults they like best. Kids have radar for Relaters. They love Mister Rogers but pooh-pooh Dr. Who. They love your silly, underachieving black-sheep cousin, but can't stand your fabulously successful, stick-in-the-mud "pride of the family" lawyer brother.

"All I ever wanted was to be a kid and play," croons folksinger John Gorka in his song "Land of the Bottom Line." Such sentiment inflames the establishment, but Relaters rarely care about establishment values. Unlike their workaholic peers, they know how to let their hair down. They love to party and celebrate, and have a way of turning ordinary events into fun adventures. Shopping becomes an excuse to try on wild clothing or sample exotic new foods; walking the dog a chance to hob-nob with the neighbors and pick wildflowers.

In "Redemption," Guinan tries to get Worf to lighten up while she creams him in a target shoot game. "Klingons do not laugh," he says, but she takes issue, doing everything she can to help him find his funny bone. Lwaxana Troi also knows the value of having a good time. She winces when she sees Worf trying to turn his son Alexander into a responsible adult. To Worf's utter horror, she whisks the child away to romp around naked in a colony of free spirits.

Adult society expects "responsible" behavior from its members; real-life Relaters sometimes get into trouble by letting their playful impulses run free. That is, unless they end up in show business, which many Relaters do. Showbiz offers a professional playground for Relaters, a haven from the dreary world of consequence. Orson Welles, the actor and director, once referred to the RKO movie studio as "the biggest electric train set any boy ever had." For many years, musician Elton John wore crazy costumes and outrageous eyeglasses—and got great publicity mileage out of it. Early in his career Elvis wriggled around on stage so unabashedly that the stodgy Ed Sullivan ordered his cameramen to shoot Elvis from the waist up only. Liz Taylor married every man she ever met. It's no secret that most of us deeply enjoy hearing about the escapades of showbiz personalities. We vicariously live out our wildest fantasies through them, and so we patronize them generously, though we wouldn't dare to emulate them.

Unlike these showbiz types, most Relaters live much more mundane lives, staying well within the boundaries of decorum. In fact, their exuberant, sometimes quirky, always caring approach to life wins many friends in an amazingly diverse cross-section of humanity. After all, who can resist someone who showers you with affection and hangs on your every word? Someone who bares his or her own soul to you without hesitation? Relaters often have circles of admirers form around them. Walt Whitman became the key man in a group of intellectuals that met regularly; Oprah Winfrey was voted president of her high school class; and people still wait for Elvis to return from his grave.

Lwaxana Troi eventually falls for virtually every testosterone-based life form aboard the *Enterprise*. (The notable exception is "Mr. Woof"; he's too serious for her blood.) Like Lwaxana, all Relaters have an abundance of libido and can't live without love. They always have someone to shower their affections on, and if they don't, they pursue a partner with great determination and energy. Their efforts usually pay off; Relaters tend to have great success in finding romance. In fact, they sometimes go overboard, letting amorous pursuits completely dominate their lives.

Famous Relaters with a bit too much love to give include Warren Beatty, who romanced literally hundreds of women before finally falling for Annette Bening; Liz Taylor, now on her eighth husband; Sidney Simon, the hugging therapist who couldn't stop at a mere embrace; Wilt Chamberlain, who claims that he had sex with thousands of women; and King Henry VIII, who tore his country apart to pursue his amorous interests.

In spite of their ardent crusades, Relaters become extraordinarily devoted partners if they find the right mates. Once they settle down, they bestow affection easily and profusely, will do anything to make their partners laugh, and get tremendous joy from giving emotionally and materially to their beloved. In fact, Relaters deluge their mates with adoration.

On *Star Trek*, Bashir flirts with a never-ending string of attractions, but when he finally falls for Melora, he treats her with great tenderness and affection. In the same way, Lwaxana shows great devotion to anyone she sets her sights on, as long as the feeling lasts.

The most romantic of all types, Relaters can get downright sentimental. If you want to get chocolates on Valentine's Day and love poems on your birthday, find a Relater to romance you. Your Relater partner will listen to your problems, always have a shoulder ready for you, learn your deepest secrets and most heinous crimes—and still adore you. Just don't ask for space, because Relaters won't understand your need for time alone. In fact, if you withdraw to get some breathing room, watch out! Hell hath no fury like a Relater scorned. That's why Relaters often fare best in relationships with other Relaters; both partners share an unrelenting need for intimacy.

Comedians George Burns and Gracie Allen, a famous Relater pair, did everything together. They lived together, played together, and worked together on radio and television for nearly four decades. Gracie died in 1964, but to this day, George, almost a century old, still visits her crypt every week and talks to her about every little thing happening in his life. The Relater's fire of passion, once lit, never dies.

Well-known Relater couples include Robert and Elizabeth Barrett

Browning, who wrote timeless love ballads to each other ("How do I love thee? Let me count the ways. . . ."); pianist Yanni and his wife, Linda Evans, who swoon over each other on public television with such ardor that they embarrass viewers; John Tesh and Connie Selleca; Paul and Linda McCartney; Tristan and Isolde; Romeo and Juliet.

At work, as in all aspects of their lives, Relaters let their passions lead them. If their career feeds their passions, they work exceptionally hard—although they always leave space for their personal life. Relaters need time to play and dream, even if they love their work. Otherwise, they become despondent and useless. In fact, Relaters approach their work as play. The corporate culture rarely encourages on-the-job fun or a laid-back mentality, and so they usually do better in other types of environments such as non-profit settings, arts organizations, schools, fitness centers, or hospitals. If a Relater does end up in a structured corporate environment, it better be one where human factors matter a lot.

Ben and Jerry, kings of the ice cream empire, provide a case study in how Relaters operate within a traditional business environment. Their company actually employs a "Minister of Joy," and celebrates holidays like "Elvis Day" and "Barry Manilow Day." All staff members get to bring home six pints of ice cream every week, a rather unusual benefit. Top executives make salaries only slightly higher than those of factory workers to promote equality within the corporation. And from the very start, the company has donated 7.5 percent of its profits to various charities.

During its heyday, Digital Equipment Corporation also maintained a Relater environment. Employees were encouraged to bring family members onto the staff, an almost unheard of business practice. Instead of the traditional hierarchical structure, the company organized itself around teams, with almost all work done in groups. From their own desks, employees could access an international online network that allowed them to exchange recipes, travel ideas, poems, and virtually any other information with DEC friends worldwide. And when the company started to lose money in a big way, the administration refused to lay any-body off—a humane but unfortunate business decision, according to experts. Even now, when declining revenues force the layoff of thousands of employees, the company provides an incredibly generous severance package.

What happens when Relaters get in trouble? Can they love their way out of danger? Or does their playful, affectionate nature crumble under duress?

In "Menage a Troi," Lwaxana gets kidnapped by a Ferengi who's smitten with her. He also snags Deanna and Riker to hold as bargaining chips. Although Lwaxana finds her Ferengi admirer absolutely repugnant, she plays along with his advances and finally agrees to stay with him for the rest of her life—if he promises to let Deanna and Riker go. Lwaxana willingly sacrifices her own happiness to buy her daughter's freedom. Similarly, in "Half a Life," Lwaxana accompanies Timicin to his ritual suicide. Her heart breaks over such a wasteful death, yet she overcomes her pain so that at Timicin's fateful moment she'll be there by his side. For a seemingly flaky lech, she sure does know how to give of herself.

Like Lwaxana, highly developed Relaters possess a most remarkable willingness to sacrifice for those they love. When cornered, they try to make contact with the soul of their attacker, to establish some form of communication. If that doesn't work, they do whatever they humanly can for those they love.

And so, Relaters at their best exemplify love in action. Like Mother Teresa, who spends all of her time and life energy ministering to the most destitute, sick, and degraded of people, hero Relaters give of themselves selflessly, expecting no reward. They draw strength from an inner source so deep and vast that it leaves the rest of us gaping in wonder.

QUICK RELATER PROFILE

A RELATER'S FAVORITE MOVIES:
Gone with the Wind; Moonstruck; A Thousand Clowns; It's a Wonderful Life; Close Encounters of the Third Kind; Crossing Delancey; Big; E.T.; Sleepless in Seattle; Love Story; Casablanca

A RELATER'S FAVORITE BOOKS:
The Prophet, by Kahlil Gibran; *Lord of the Rings,* by J. R. R. Tolkien; *The Road Less Traveled,* by M. Scott Peck; any romance novel; *The Little Prince,* by Antoine de Saint-Exupéry; anything by Amy Tan or Anne Tyler; *Random Acts of Kindness*

A RELATER'S IDEA OF A GREAT VACATION:
Any trip that involves taking along at least a few friends; visiting Disney World/Epcot; two weeks at Club Med

A RELATER'S MOTTOS:
"Love makes the world go 'round."

"Make hay while the sun shines."

"I feel your pain."

GOOD JOBS FOR RELATERS:
Counselor; teacher; social director; minister; rabbi; actor; pop musician; personnel director; camp director; nurse; consultant

WHAT YOU'LL FIND IN A RELATER'S OFFICE:
Photos of family and friends; paintings of people; stuffed animals and toys; cartoons; speed dial with friends' numbers; calendar of birthdays; pictures drawn by kids

A RELATER'S WORST NIGHTMARES:
Getting stuck alone on a desert island; becoming an accountant

TELLTALE RELATER BEHAVIORS:
Gives you a big hug when you meet; openly enjoys parties and group outings; goes out to lunch with friends instead of brown-bagging it; makes you feel comfortable immediately; invites you

over to dinner or out to lunch before you even learn his or her name; laughs easily

What Relaters Wear:

Clothes intended to please other people. Relaters dress well, although they tend toward the casual and slightly unconventional. A button that says "Have a Nice Day" is a dead giveaway; so are T-shirts with jokes on them.

Relater Songs:

"You've Got a Friend"; "You're a Friend of Mine"; "I'll Be There for You"; "Lean on Me"; "Old Friends"; "Tea for Two"

Famous Relaters:

Mister Rogers; Leo Buscaglia; Mother Teresa; Click and Clack of Car Talk; Jerry Brown; Ben & Jerry; Bill Clinton; Pete Seeger; Billy Crystal; Eleanor Roosevelt; Judy Garland; Peter Pan; the Pied Piper; the Seven Dwarfs

11

A LITTLE GUINAN KEEPS YOUR

ULCER IN CHECK (BUT TOO

MUCH CAN GIVE YOU THE GOUT)

Al Gore had presidential aspirations, but he had to settle for the second place spot. Why did this man—with no skeletons in his closet, no enemies, no gluttony or infidelity to mar his record—come in behind his less sterling running mate? Because he also had no personality. "Loosen Up, Al," screamed a headline in *Southern Magazine*. People respected Al, but they didn't like him. "He's stiff . . . pedantic . . . programmed," said writer Curtis Wilkie, and most Americans nodded their heads in agreement.

Then one day, Al expressed himself. He danced on the *Today* show, smashed an ashtray on Letterman, and pulled no punches in a debate with Ross Perot. He revealed that his family had benefited from therapy and talked about the trauma of his son's near-fatal injury. Suddenly, the public loved him. "Al Gore, Bore No More," a *Washington Post* headline announced.

Al Gore showed us that to win friends in this world, you need to display emotion. Still, many of us submerge our feelings, trying to forge ahead with the business of life. Intimacy makes us squirm, blatant emotionalism sends us running, and we rarely let loose except when drunk. Unfortunately, suppressing feelings takes its toll. In Al Gore's case the price was merely a political setback, but the less lucky among us get sick, go nuts, or end up alone. Psychologists tell us that when you don't let out your anger, you get depressed; doctors claim that keeping emotions inside can lead to a host of physical ailments: ulcers, headaches, greater vulnerability to infection.

Of course, most of us *do* cry and express our feelings—if we can find a private time and place to do so. We certainly *never* cry in public, in front of others. We keep our emotions secret, not wanting to show people how much we hurt or love or fear. In fact, we treat our emotions almost like sinful things that nobody else can know about. In doing so, we may well sabotage our chances for happiness.

Look at what happens to Spock because he ignores his feelings. In the classic episode "This Side of Paradise," he gets blasted by spores from a plant that stimulates emotions, falls in love with a woman named Leila and frolics around with her, even dangling upside down from a tree. When Kirk finds an antidote and yanks Spock out of his reverie, Spock says, "All I know is that for the first time in my life . . . I was happy." Poor Spock! Although his usual denial of emotions lets him avoid the agonies of life, it also keeps him from knowing real joy.

A recent story in the news shows what happens when you stuff your feelings inside and keep them there. Dozens of New York cops went on a drunken rampage while visiting Washington for, of all things, a memorial service. Everyone knows that police officers face unimaginable stresses on the job: They deal with crime, human suffering, life-threatening violence. They often must choke back their own feelings in order to cope. Unfortunately, these officers, desperately needing release, found it only with chemical assistance, and then ended up in big trouble.

The novel, also a film, *Remains of the Day* presents a similarly sad story. The heroine, a maid in a proper British household, loves the butler. She never dares to discuss her feelings with him, or even to admit her ardor to herself. Meanwhile, he won't face his feelings for her, believing that proper butlers should be one-hundred-percent devoted to their jobs, not dilly-dallying around with romance. And so, these two people never consummate their passion for each other, instead living lonely, frustrated lives.

Like the butler and the maid, we often don't even *know* what we feel. Who has time to "get in touch with feelings" these days? When something really infuriates us, we know it, of course. When we feel tremendous joy we know that, too. But we don't know why we have intestinal distress from day to day, or anxiety attacks, or a bad attitude. We blame the moon, the traffic, the bills. But often, something deep down inside really bothers us, and we don't even know what it is. Even worse, we don't want to know. We just want to make it through the day without feeling pain. Getting in touch with emotions may lead to unpleasant things, and we have enough to worry about. So when emotions nag at us—when we continue to chafe, for example, about that rude remark our aunt made at the last family gathering, or when we swallow the indignity of having our boss chew us out in front of the whole department—we just shove the feelings back inside, to be dealt with "later."

What happens to these unacknowledged feelings? They turn into cancer inside of us, figuratively—and even literally. Numerous studies show that people who freely express emotions don't get sick as often as other people, plus they recover more quickly. In *Healing and the Mind,* by Bill Moyers, contributor Dr. Michael Lerner writes of a scientific study of patients with malignant melanoma in which it was found that patients who expressed their feelings had more immune activity at the site of their lesions than patients who didn't express their feelings.

You've probably had the experience of avoiding your own feelings and then ending up with headaches or stomach aches or back problems. If you get in the habit of suppressing your emotions, you can make yourself seriously ill. And so, for health reasons if for none other, you need to get in touch with your emotions and let them show.

In the *Star Trek* pilot episode, "The Cage," Captain Pike discovers that he can elude his Talosian captors by feeling anger. Whenever he gets mad, they can't read him. Similarly, in "Plato's Stepchildren," the dwarf Alexander breaks free of his enslavement by throwing a fit. In the *Next Generation* episode "The Outrageous Okona," love between sweethearts from warring planets finally stops an age-old war. And in "Chain of Command," Picard keeps his wits by constantly exploding at his Cardassian torturer.

These episodes offer a clear message: Showing emotions can get you out of a jam. This theme isn't unique to *Star Trek*. Emotional displays save the day in many books, movies, parables, even fairy tales. In *Sleeping Beauty*, the prince loves the heroine out of a deathly slumber. A similar thing happens in *Snow White*. In *Rapunzel*, the heroine's tears of joy heal the blind prince. And in *Beauty and the Beast*, the heroine's grief at finding the Beast near death saves his life and transforms him into a prince.

Fairy tales offer metaphors for real-life truths, as do tales from *Star Trek*. But exactly *how* do you implement the wisdom of these stories? How can you let your feelings show without making people cringe and without making yourself too vulnerable? Easy. Just express the fact that you *have* feelings without dripping all over people. You can say, "I feel sad," without sobbing hysterically. You can declare "I love you" without breaking into song. You've got to give people breathing room.

When Barbara Walters interviewed Michael Landon shortly before he died, he openly expressed his sadness at having cancer and having to leave his family behind. He even got a tear in his eye. Viewers sympathized with him, gained strength and inspiration from him, cried for him. If Michael had let the one tear become a flood of tears, he would have scared viewers off. Instead, he maintained his own dignity, and so touched people deeply, in an unforgettable way.

It takes courage to express emotions openly like Michael Landon did, because we fear getting trampled on if we do so. We think we're the only ones who get hurt so easily, who feel so sensitive. Relaters know better. They realize that *everybody* has fears and hurts and secret delights. They take the risk of exposing themselves because they crave closeness with other people, and know that if they talk about their own experiences, they may touch a chord deep within others.

To connect with people, you need to let them know you. That means making yourself vulnerable, risking rejection. True, whenever you show your heart to someone else, you risk getting it tromped on. On the other hand, Relaters end up with more friends than the rest of us, and their friendships tend to be deeper and more fulfilling. Why? Not only because they allow people to get close to them, but also because they make it their business to get close to people.

If you want to find friends and lovers, you can't sit around hoping God will deliver them to your doorstep. Would you wait around passively if you wanted a new car, hoping that luck or fate would bring it to you? Of course not. You need to go after what you want. You must invoke your inner Relater and thrust yourself in front of people, showing real interest in them.

Guinan reaches out to people nonstop, never worrying about getting rejected, and happily, her efforts usually pay off. When Ro Laren asks Guinan to leave her alone in "Ensign Ro," Guinan refuses and sits down at Ro's table. She converts Ro into a friend in spite of her objections, just by constantly asserting that they have a bond. She uses the same tactics with Wesley when he wants time alone to think in "The Child," getting him to talk to her about his troubles. She even corners Worf, urging him in "Yesterday's Enterprise" to lighten up and to get a girlfriend.

If you don't feel satisfied with your current friendships or love life, you need to develop Guinan's dedication to making friends. Ask yourself how much effort you actually make to befriend others. How often do you invite people to your house, or out to lunch, or to do things with you? What if they refuse the first few times? Do you try again? Do you openly tell them you care about them, seek opportunities to ask about their hopes and dreams? And if people do reject you, do you retreat into isolation, or do you try, try again—and again—with someone else?

According to the gospel of John and Paul, in the end, the love you take is equal to the love you make. If love flows from you like a fountain, you'll be swimming in intimate relationships. Watch the people you know who have lots of friends. See how they put themselves in front of others, how they offer their friendship so easily. Relaters have no big secret except this: They show interest in people, care about people, and don't fear making the first move (or the second).

In his classic book *How to Win Friends and Influence People*, Dale Carnegie wrote:

> Many of the sweetest memories of my childhood cluster a round a little yellow-haired dog with a stub tail. "Tippy" had a perfect technique for making people like him. He liked people himself—and his interest was so sincere and so genuine that I couldn't keep from liking him and loving him in return. Tippy knew that you can make more friends in two months by becoming genuinely interested in other people than you can in two years by trying to get other people interested in you.

If you lack Tippy's charm and people just don't warm up to you, do what Tippy would do. If one person rejects you, run to the next person with great interest and affection, and you'll soon develop quite a fan club—guaranteed.

The same story holds if you want more intimacy with the friends and lovers you already have. You can't wait for them to make the first move or to change in some fundamental way. You need to blast the people you care about with love. Don't worry about getting it back—because you may not. On the other hand, your love may trigger a new level of trust in others and may make them feel safe enough to change themselves and to love you back.

Lwaxana Troi sure doesn't care what people think about her. She just dishes out affection all over the place, never worrying about getting rejected. Although many do spurn her advances, her efforts ultimately pay off. She finds love with Timicin, makes friends with Odo and Alexander, and in fact, changes their lives. In the end, she even wins the respect of those who once thought her flaky, as in "Menage a Troi," when she shows her true mettle to Deanna and Riker by sacrificing herself to save them.

In 1994, *Forrest Gump* became the highest grossing non-science-fiction film in history. Why? People adore the all-heart, no-mind leading character. Forrest Gump gives everything he's got—from his chocolates to his fortunes to his homilies ("Stupid is as stupid does") to anyone willing to accept his gifts. Gump is pure Relater, and everyone loves him for it.

When you think about the people who move you, who inspire you, whom you value the most, who comes to mind? People with vast stores of knowledge, or people with huge hearts? We aspire to greatness, thinking we'll affect the world with our distinguished accomplishments. Our deeds may earn us a headline in a newspaper, but such tributes are usually discarded in the next day's trash. It's giving of ourselves that wins us a permanent place in the hearts and souls of our fellow Earthlings. We never forget people who affect our hearts and we don't forget what they teach us—though we may soon forget the great deeds of big shots we encounter. As spiritual teacher Sri Chinmoy says, "Greatness is a matter of a moment, goodness is the work of a lifetime."

In the *Next Generation* episode "Loud as a Whisper," a deaf and mute ambassador named Riva tragically loses the "chorus" of helpers who communicate for him. Riva's grief at losing his friends paralyzes him; he refuses to complete a diplomatic mission and basically opts out of life. Deanna Troi counsels him in spite of his objections, helping him to find another way to communicate, turning his disability into an asset. You can bet that Riva values Deanna's kindness, compassion, and wisdom more dearly than anything he receives from the big shots of the universe whom he routinely meets.

If you want to make an enduring difference in people's lives, as Deanna did for Riva, you need to mobilize your Relater. The most highly developed Relaters give ceaselessly not only to their own circle of family and friends, but to the world at large. In this century, numerous Relaters have become famous for their tireless work on behalf of humanity. Mother Teresa shows overflowing generosity of spirit. Like many true Relaters, she sees the world as one family, and acts accordingly. "The poor are our brothers and sisters," says Mother Teresa; members of the order she founded take a vow to serve the poor and to see those they help as the embodiment of Christ. Mother Teresa received the Nobel Peace Prize in 1979.

Another famous Relater who served the world tirelessly and won hearts around the globe was Eleanor Roosevelt, who used her position as the wife of the President to campaign for humanitarian causes. She supported a youth employment program, fought for racial equality (resigning from the Daughters of the American Revolution when the group refused to allow black diva Marian Anderson to sing in its hall), visited soldiers during World War II, campaigned for desegregation of the armed forces, and lobbied on behalf of Jews displaced by the war. After her husband died, she served as a delegate to the United Nations, continuing to fight for human rights.

Other examples include Albert Schweitzer, Jimmy Carter (in his post-presidency days), and comedian Dick Gregory, who brought joy and laughter to many with his barbed wit and insightful comments at the height of the civil rights movement, and who has since devoted his energies to helping others in need. In the 1960s and 1970s he was an ardent campaigner for justice and human dignity. Later, as the operator of a nutrition clinic in the Bahamas, he came to the rescue of a 1,200-pound man on Long Island, counseling him about weight loss, supervising his diet, and picking up the tab for his medical bills.

If you want to make an enduring difference in people's lives, you too need to mobilize your Relater. We're not saying that you have to put on a sackcloth, smudge yourself with ashes, and go establish a medical clinic in the hinterlands. But you might need to adjust the fine tuning on your emotional radar to get a better picture of human needs and feelings.

Finally—but no less importantly—you need to wake up your Relater in order to have fun and to keep perspective on life. In these workaholic times, you can easily wear yourself down trying to keep up with demands placed on you, trying to be perfect. The Relater knows when to skip work and go to the amusement park, when to lighten up. Relaters show great kindness not only to others, but also to themselves. They let themselves enjoy life. They put first things first. Like Lwaxana Troi, they know that "life's true gift is to enjoy enjoyment."

❋

The Relater qualities—compassion, empathy, friendliness, joyfulness—seem so benign that it's hard to imagine having *too much* Relater. And yet, you *can* give too much, party too much, and feel too much for your own good. To become the well-rounded person you want to be, you've got to maintain all the heroic qualities in balance. The Relater aspect is no exception.

Relaters gone overboard often suffer enormously. We all know people who want love so badly that they even pursue doomed relationships. Judging by the letters that appear in Ann Landers's column, huge numbers of us fall in love with unavailable married people, or choose wildly inappropriate mates, or can't break free from dysfunctional families. Although Lwaxana Troi has a huge heart and admirable Relater traits, she's constantly in danger of going too far. In the *Star Trek* universe, she's the prototype "woman who loves too much," continually chasing after men who don't return her love. She never learns, pursuing Picard in spite of his complete uninterest in her, and in "Cost of Living," makes plans to marry a haughty, cold, humorless ambassador. (Fortunately, her straight-laced fiancé calls off the marriage when Troi, honoring Betazoid custom—and her own ambivalence—shows up for the wedding in the nude.)

It's a beautiful thing to keep your heart open, but you have to know when to raise shields and protect yourself. A children's story called *The Giving Tree,* by Shel Silverstein, plainly illustrates what happens when you lavish too much love on the wrong people. Over the years the tree offers its gifts unstintingly to a selfish and unappreciative young boy. The tree gives him its fruits to eat, its branches to swing on, then its wood so he can build a house. Finally, depleted, the tree has nothing left to give but a stump for the boy—now an old man—to sit on. In the end, the boy discovers that he loves the tree, but only after the tree is completely spent. Likewise, if you give and give to the wrong people, if you don't apply discrimination or common sense, you'll become as depleted as that tree.

Loving indiscriminately can lead to more trouble than a wounded heart. Overboard Relaters tend to get too attached to their work, to their country, even to their possessions. For instance, when companies downsize, Relaters often cling to their workplace even as their jobs become obsolete. While their less emotional colleagues job-hunt, learn new skills, and prepare for the future, the overdeveloped Relaters ignore reality until it's too late. That's what happened to Luciano Pavarotti. Pavarotti is a gonzo Relater; once in an interview he said, "I love people. I genuinely love everybody." He often extends his personal appearances far beyond the scheduled two hours, signing autographs and shaking hands until he personally greets everyone who came to see him has that opportunity. But Pavarotti's generosity worked against him at least once. He missed too many performances at the Lyric Opera of Chicago and got fired in 1989. He felt such loyalty to the opera company that even he, the great

Pavarotti, didn't secure another singing engagement in time to save face.

People who love indiscriminately may also become too attached to their homeland, even when it becomes unsafe. In the classic episode "The Mark of Gideon," the inhabitants of a horribly overpopulated planet won't go elsewhere, although crowded conditions have virtually eliminated privacy and people can barely move. They sit back while the leader decides to take care of the problem by introducing a lethal disease that will kill off half of the population. The Gideons would rather die than go. Likewise, in pre-war Germany, many Jews and other vulnerable people refused to leave the country, although they had warning of things to come and had ample time to leave. They stayed because they were loyal Germans who loved their country. They believed patriotism would spare them. They were sadly wrong.

When not suffering from their misguided attachments, overdeveloped Relaters feel miserable because of their extreme emotional sensitivity. They live to please other people, and when they fail, they fall apart. They care far too much what people think of them. Even the slightest rejection or mood changes in others can devastate them, and they may compensate by jumping into self-destructive behaviors, especially drinking or taking drugs. Of all the types, Relaters are the most addiction-prone, even more so because they love to party.

In Hollywood, overdeveloped Relaters find lots of company. Marilyn Monroe and Judy Garland buried their hurts in promiscuity and addictions that ultimately killed them. Likewise, Janis Joplin became famous for her one-night stands and addiction to Southern Comfort. She ultimately died from a heroin overdose. Elvis also died an inglorious, drug-induced death. Richard Pryor got so strung out on drugs that he accidentally torched himself when a lighter exploded while he was trying to smoke freebase cocaine; he nearly died from the burns. All these people are known for their highly sensitive natures, gregarious personalities, and desperate desire to win approval from the public-at-large as well as from their intimates.

Relaters don't like to refuse anybody anything, because they want so much to please people. When offered a chance to party, or to do someone a favor, or to give a little more of themselves, they have trouble saying no. When asked to stay late at work, they do it without complaint. When asked to drive the neighbor to the airport at midnight, they do that, too. They babysit for the neighbors' kids and dogs and in-laws. When asked to collect for the Boy Scouts, for cerebral palsy, for any cause that comes down the pike, they take up the challenge. They sometimes get so over-burdened with the things they do for others that they find they have no time left for themselves, for the fun that their Relater nature so desperately needs.

When taken to extremes, the Relater's desire to please others can become dangerous. Woody Allen's movie *Zelig* portrays a character so anxious to be liked that he takes on the characteristics of everyone he meets, from President Roosevelt to Adolf Hitler. Zelig will do anything to win a friend. Although the film seems far-fetched, the same thing happens every day in real life. People who are so desperate to join a group but who can't find a healthy outlet will join youth gangs, or fringe political movements, or ter-rorist groups. In order to fit in and be liked, group members mimic each other, even when it means doing perilous, terrible things.

Out-of-balance Relaters crave pleasure as much as they crave friendship. In their fervent pursuit of anything that feels good, they disregard any obstacle in their way, including the law. All Relaters have trouble taking rules seriously, but overboard Relaters go one step beyond, flaunting the law and sometimes landing in serious trouble. They drive too fast, ingest any sub-stance that makes them feel good, steal what they can't buy, and do anything that will give them a rush.

Unfortunately, that rush sometimes comes from exploiting other people. In the classic episode "Mudd's Women," the greedy Harry Mudd makes a fortune by supplying remote parts of the galaxy with attractive women, whom he kidnaps and administers beauty-enhancing drugs to. Mudd reappears in a later episode, this time ruling an entire race of robots who eventually get disillusioned with his lust, greed, and gluttony. Mudd is a prime specimen of the misguided Relater. He doesn't really want to harm anyone; he just wants nonstop pleasure for himself, at almost any cost. In spite of his perversions and crimes, Mudd manages to evoke sympathy in viewers. Relaters have a remarkable way of remaining likeable, even at their most twisted.

Why did the O. J. Simpson murder trial become the longest running and most compelling news story of the decade? Because people couldn't get over the fact that this most affable of guys might have committed such a base, gruesome crime. O.J. exuded Relater charm, even from his courtroom perch, and so intrigues people endlessly. Likewise, Ted Kennedy managed to hold a seat in the Senate for decades, despite the Chappaquiddick scandal, his notorious reputation as a womanizer, and his love of the bottle. Ted knows how to work a crowd; he somehow charms people into forgiving his dissolute tendencies. "The poor guy," we think, "he lost two brothers and really has it rough." Others would surely have been impeached, but not Ted Kennedy, Relater supreme.

Meanwhile, Ted's political enemy Ronald Reagan danced around the Iran-Contra problem, losing no popularity points in spite of his flagrant evasion of the laws of the country. Instead, the public saw in him a concerned grandfather figure who embodied wisdom and kindness. Can you imagine how the public would have viewed the same scandal if Richard Nixon or Lyndon Johnson had been at the helm? Reagan's Relater charm saved his hide.

At their worst, Relaters gone bonkers become raving egotists. In their pursuit of anything that feels good, they discover the joys of asserting their superiority. If other people won't praise them, entertain them, and give them love, they do it for themselves, to excess.

In the "The Schizoid Man," a brilliant but terminally ill scientist, Dr. Ira Graves, injects his consciousness into Data's mind at the point of his death. He believes his superior intelligence gives him the right to take over Data's mind, but the crew catches on when Data starts acting out-of-character, especially when he delivers an effusive, adoring eulogy at Graves's funeral.

At the far end of the scale, when Relaters go overboard into the land of perversion, when their egotism intersects with their love of pleasure, they become shameless lechers. The media bombards us with stories about people who think their own greatness gives them license to seduce, exploit, and even rape others. From Baghwan Shree Rajneesh, who preached open sexuality as a means to greater awareness, to Jim Bakker, the evangelist who seduced his church secretary, to Clarence Thomas, who allegedly made inane sexual comments to co-workers, to any one of the numerous pedophile clergymen who put the fear of God into the helpless boys and girls entrusted to their spiritual guidance—these people abuse positions of power, and yet invariably seem surprised—even outraged—when caught.

And so you see, even the heroic Relater qualities can turn sour if overdeveloped. Most of us fall on the other side of the equation, though—we need more Relater, not less. As life on this planet speeds up and we get ever busier, we take less and less time out for love and for fun. We need to remember how to play, how to listen to people, how to care for others, how to care for ourselves.

The Relater gets out of hand only when other qualities are neglected. You need to both give of yourself *and* take time out for fun; to love other people *as well as yourself*. If you don't love yourself, you'll become obsessed with pumping up your own ego or forcing others to love you. If you give of yourself but don't take time out to play, you'll eventually hit the wall and become obsessed with grabbing pleasure however you can. Acting like a Relater means manifesting *all* the Relater qualities.

The exercises in the next chapter will help you to invoke your Relater and to express it properly.

12

EXERCISES TO DEVELOP YOUR

INNER GUINAN

Wallflowers, put on your dancing shoes! It's time to make friends and have fun. To boldly live like you've never lived before, you've got to stop hiding out, feeling lonely and misunderstood. You've got to reach out to people, express your feelings, and listen to your heart as well as to your intelligence. If you don't, how will you ever develop real friendships or get intimate with your mate? How will you even win a mate?

This chapter helps you learn the simple relationship secrets that Guinan knows so well. You'll practice listening with empathy, speaking with compassion, and communicating your true feelings. You'll practice acting like a loving, all-around good person instead of like a toad.

So read on. The world wants and needs you. Practice the Relater exercises on the next pages and referring often to the Relater Checklist that follows as you do, so you'll see that it's true.

RELATER CHECKLIST

❑ Watch *Star Trek* Relaters.
❑ Smile and laugh.
❑ Make warm eye contact.
❑ Loosen up.
❑ Gesture.
❑ Reach out and touch someone.
❑ Smile.
❑ Be intensely attentive.
❑ Vary volume and pitch when you speak.
❑ Ask questions.
❑ Use colorful language.
❑ Listen!
❑ Share your feelings.
❑ Empathize.

EXERCISE 1

Look Like a Relater

Practice this exercise with another person; you can't relate by yourself. Find someone you don't feel self-conscious with so you can get feedback on how you're doing. Refer to *Star Trek* episodes any time you need help capturing the Relater look.

1. Warm up by watching *Star Trek* episodes featuring Relaters. Good choices include McCoy in the classic episodes "For the World Is Hollow and I Have Touched the Sky"; "The Empath"; "This Side of Paradise" (even Spock becomes a Relater in this one); Lwaxana in the *Next Generation* episodes "Half a Life" and "Cost of Living"; or Guinan in "Ensign Ro," "The Dauphin," or "The Outrageous Okona." Other good choices include any episodes featuring Deanna Troi, Bashir, or Kes.

2.   Go casual. Relaters project ease and approachability. Relax. Breathe deeply, and let the muscles in your neck, shoulders, and face relax.

3.   Let "the moon hit your eye like a big pizza pie." Use soft, affectionate eye contact. Your eyes let others know how you feel about them. Let your fondness for the person with you show in your eyes. Don't stare, but do try to see the other person fully by looking warmly into his or her eyes.

4.   Gesture. Relaters use their bodies to express their feelings. Let your hands and limbs move with your emotions.

5.   Reach out. Touch others and let them touch you. Relaters love physical contact, and they routinely touch to communicate. A friendly pat on the back, a sympathetic touch on the arm, a warm hug all express more than words alone. Try to incorporate one of these forms of contact into your conversation with your helper during this exercise.

6.   Say "cheese." Relaters enjoy people and life, and they let their enjoyment show by smiling a lot.

7.   Be attentive. Face your partner and give him or her all your attention. Turn off the TV, don't hum with the radio, don't putter while your friend pours his or her heart out.

EXERCISE 2

Talk Like a Relater

This exercise will help you to talk to others with empathy and concern. If you get impatient with people who don't get right to the point, or if you have trouble talking to people about their feelings (or about yours), you'll find this exercise particularly helpful. Try applying this exercise to different situations:

❑   offering sympathy to a sick friend
❑   asking someone why she's angry at you
❑   disagreeing with a relative
❑   telling your partner what you like about him or her

1.   Warm up by listening to McCoy, Lwaxana, Guinan, Kes, or Deanna Troi. Before you begin, watch episodes featuring the *Star Trek* Relaters. Pay careful attention to their body language, facial expressions, and vocal inflections. Notice how Relaters express feelings with their bodies as well as with words.

2.   Let your voice change as your feelings change. Relaters vary pitch and tone when they speak. Practice varying the volume of your voice to reflect the intensity of your emotions. Try different tones to express sadness, joy, anger, frustration, jealousy, sorrow, fear, and other emotions.

3.   Enjoy a belly laugh. Relaters see humor in almost everything and so laugh freely.

4.   Use spicy language. Relaters enjoy the act of communicating, and so often use colorful figures of speech. Think of communication as an art form. Try using images that convey your whole experience (physical, emotional, psychological).

5.   Play Twenty Questions. Relaters really want to know what others feel, and don't begin by assuming that they know. Asking good questions helps you to truly understand other people and invites communication. Use open-ended questions like: "What do you think about . . ." or "How do you feel about . . ." or "What are you concerned about?"

6.   Empathize. Show that you accept the other person's thoughts and feelings without judging. Don't offer advice; give support only. You can say things like: "It must be very hard for you right now" or "I don't blame you for feeling that way" or "How can I better understand what you're going through?"

7.   Open ears, shut mouth. Listen, no matter how hard it is to hear what the other person is saying. Paraphrase what you hear—without judgment or criticism—to confirm that you properly understand the other person's meaning and to show that you care. Of all Relater skills, this one is the most rare and difficult. Very few people know how to truly listen.

8. Share your own feelings. Don't make your feelings a comment about the other person. State them as your own. Not "You're a jerk," but "What you just said made me angry."

9. Remain upbeat. Accentuate the positive. Relaters know that a kind or encouraging word goes a long way. Compliment others when they deserve it. Tell people when they make you happy. Focusing on the positive and communicating your positive feelings will improve your outlook, intensify your friendships, and reduce your blood pressure.

EXERCISE 3

Respond Like a Relater

In order to relate, you have to talk to others in a way that invites communication. You must show that you care, that you are listening, and that you understand what the other person is going through.

Imagine that someone you know said each of the statements below. What Relater-talk would you use to respond? Write your responses below. This exercise gives you practice in thinking like a Relater.

1. "I'm always stuck with these menial jobs."

   Your response:

   _____

   _____

   _____

   _____

2. "I felt like I did a good job on the report that you criticized."

    Your response:

    _____

    _____

    _____

    _____

3. "I guess that you and I just have a personality conflict."

    Your response:

    _____

    _____

    _____ _____

    _____

4. "Don't talk to me. Today's not my day."

    Your response:

    _____

    _____

    _____

    _____

5. "I was promoted to manager last week."

   Your response:

   _____

   _____

   _____

   _____

6. "I'm really angry. This new policy stinks."

   Your response:

   _____

   _____

   _____

   _____

7. "You're always pushing your ideas on the rest of us."

   Your response:

   _____

   _____

   _____

   _____

8.   "We would have the job done already if Sally wasn't goofing off."

Your response:

_____

_____

_____

EXERCISE 4

Relate Your Way Through a Confrontation

In the following exercise, you'll use affirmative Relater statements, questions, listening, and sharing to develop mutual understanding and prevent a confrontation. First, you'll think through your plan of action, and then you'll role-play it with a friend.

The Scenario: Your best friend just told you that he is angry with you for snubbing him at a meeting that you both attended. He says that you were so intent on getting attention from the big shots at the meeting that you completely ignored him. In return, you feel angry that your friend would accuse you of putting ambition above friendship. In fact, you feel that your friend could have supported you instead of withdrawing into a corner.

Your Task: Use Relater-talk to get your friend to discuss the situation with you without lapsing into mutual recriminations and finger-pointing.

1.   **Prepare Relater-style responses:**

What can you say as an opening line to convince your friend that you care and want to work things out?

_____

_____

_____

_____

What questions can you ask to elicit your friend's feelings?

_____

_____

_____

_____

How can you express your feelings without blaming your friend?

_____

_____

_____

_____

2. **Role-play with a friend.** Now role-play the entire scenario, practicing your Relater responses. Ask your friend to begin the discussion by accusing you of snubbing him and playing up to the big shots. Then, put your Relater behavior into practice.

3. **When you finish, ask your friend for feedback on how you did.**

EXERCISE 5

Identify Relaters in Your Life

1. List five people you know who have strong Relater characteristics.

    _____

    _____

    _____

    _____

    _____

2. **Think about an incident you observed when a friend of yours acted like a Relater.** Perhaps you watched him show great compassion to an angry person who attacked him, or found him the only person who really listened when you needed to talk about a sensitive issue, or you noticed him having fun in a situation that other people found painful. Write down details about the Relater behaviors your friend exhibited, including how he looked, talked, and acted.

    _____

    _____

    _____

    _____

    _____

    _____

3. **Can you recall an incident in which your parents or siblings acted like Relaters?** Describe the incident, and record details about how your family member looked, sounded, and acted.

_____

_____

_____

_____

_____

4. **Recall an incident in which your boss or one of your co-workers acted like a Relater.** Again, record details about the incident and about the person's appearance, voice, and actions.

_____

_____

_____

_____

_____

5. **Now go back through each of the incidents you wrote about above, and remember how you felt as you observed your friend, your family member, your boss, or colleague act like a Relater.** Were you frightened? Proud? Intimidated?

Inspired? Write down the feelings you remember having during and after each incident. This will give you a clue about your own readiness to become a Relater.

Incident #1:

_____

_____

_____

_____

Incident #2:

_____

_____

_____

_____

Incident #3:

_____

_____

_____

_____

Role-play Exercises

This section contains exercises to help you practice your Relater skills in everyday situations. You can practice these alone, but you'll get even better results if you do them with a partner. Feel free to modify the scenarios to correspond more closely to situations that you actually face. You'll find that practicing these exercises will help you enormously when you need to act like a Relater for real.

EXERCISE 6

Where No Offspring Has Gone Before

The Situation: At this late stage in your adulthood, you suddenly realize that you never have honest, heart-to-heart conversations with your mother or father. You have certainly never talked to them about your relationship with them.

Your Task: Talk to your parent about why you don't talk more. You can do this exercise even if neither of your parents is living: Imagine that you are having this conversation before your parent died.

Suggested Episodes to Watch in Preparation:

- ❑ "Family" *(TNG):* Picard and his brother reconcile.
- ❑ "The Icarus Factor"*(TNG):* Riker has it out with his dad.
- ❑ "Journey to Babel" (classic): Spock treats his parents with Vulcan "hospitality."
- ❑ *Star Trek III* (the movie): More of Spock and Dad.

How to Proceed: Your partner should play your parent, acting distracted and not really giving you attention. Tell your parent that you would like to have a serious talk. Then, tell how you feel frustrated with your communications, not blaming or accusing, simply stating your own feelings. Also ask your parent to express his or her feelings on the subject. Tell your parent that you love him or her, and would like to have more closeness. Ask open-ended questions to understand your parent's perspective, needs, and ideas.

After practicing this role-play with your partner several times, try it for real.

EXERCISE 7

The Cardassian Patient

The Situation: Your sister hurt her back. She has been bedridden for two weeks, and is not in a good mood. You go to her house to help, but she snaps at you and makes you wish you hadn't come at all.

Your Task: Help your sister to feel better, physically *and* emotionally, in spite of her nasty behavior.

Suggested Episodes to Watch in Preparation:

- ❑ "Loud as a Whisper" *(TNG):* The ambassador Riva snaps at Troi.
- ❑ "The Child" *(TNG):* Wesley tells Guinan to leave him alone.
- ❑ "Redemption" *(TNG):* Worf tells Guinan to leave him alone.
- ❑ "Ensign Ro" *(TNG):* Ro tells Guinan to leave her alone.

How to Proceed: Ask your friend to actually lay down for this role-play, with blankets and other props to make it seem as realistic as possible. When you arrive, your friend should bombard you with a list of demands, complain bitterly about the pain, and complain how nobody was around to help when she needed help. Instead of rolling your eyes or ignoring her, sit down by her side and show sympathy. Say things like "That must have felt terrible." Ask her to describe her symptoms in detail. Listen attentively as she does so, and ask more questions to really understand what she is going through. Ask what she wants you to do first.

EXERCISE 8

Lower Shields for a Friend in Need

The Situation: Your friend just broke up with his girlfriend. They were together for two years, and he hoped that the relationship would lead to marriage. Something went wrong, and he just arrived at your house to talk about it.

Your Task: Listen empathically to what your friend says. Don't offer advice or try to make things better; just listen.

Suggested Episodes to Watch in Preparation:
- ❑ "The Forsaken" *(DS9):* Lwaxana listens when Odo describes his troubled past.
- ❑ "Cost of Living" *(TNG):* Lwaxana listens to Alexander's problems.
- ❑ "In Theory" *(TNG):* Guinan helps Data with his relationship problems.

How to Proceed: Ask your friend to role-play, arriving at your house in an extremely distraught state. Give your friend a hundred percent of your attention: Don't answer the phone or turn on the TV or pet your dog while listening to him. Ask open-ended questions to try to understand what he's going through. Restate what you hear to make sure that you understand. Realize that you can't fix this problem; you can only let your friend know that you care. When you finish, ask your friend for feedback on how you did.

Part Five

A VISION, A MISSION, AND A GREAT

SPEAKING VOICE: LIFE LESSONS

FROM THE LEADERS, KIRK,

PICARD, SISKO, AND JANEWAY

Part Two

13

SET YOUR EYES ON THE STARS

AND MAKE IT SO: THE LEADER'S CREDO

Leadership is the ability to get men to do what they don't want to do and like it.

—Harry Truman

In the final episode of *The Next Generation*, Picard time-travels into the past and arrives back at his first day as captain of the *Enterprise*. He immediately discovers a space anomaly that threatens to destroy the universe, and must undertake risky and seemingly reckless maneuvers to destroy it. The crewmembers—who don't yet know him—wonder about his ability to lead (and even about his sanity). And so, they threaten mutiny. Picard responds by delivering a speech so reassuring, so rousing, so respectful of the crew that he establishes himself as the ultimate Leader in mere seconds.

Most of us hope for a less stressful first day on the job than Picard had: Space anomaly-type problems can wait. On *his* first day, Picard faces not only unprecedented danger, but also the ire of the entire crew. Yet you can bet he wouldn't trade places with anyone. Leaders enjoy being under the gun, taking charge in crises.

To be a Leader, "You've got to want to be in charge," says Dr. Wes Roberts in *Leadership Secrets of Attila the Hun*. You need "lust for leadership." The word *lead* means to go first, and this is what Leaders must do. They take the risks for the crew; they take the heat if things go wrong. The biggest difference between Leaders and the rest of us is this: We want power and influence, but we don't want to give up anything to get it, and we certainly don't want to be on the front lines when the shooting starts. Leaders, on the other hand, rush to the front lines eagerly, more concerned about their mission than about their personal needs. Although many people like the idea of bossing around subordinates, only true Leaders welcome the headaches that go along with power.

General Robert E. Lee remained amazingly popular and respected by both his own troops and the public-at-large even after he lost the Civil War, not only for his gifts as a commander, but because he always fought on the front lines and took complete responsibility for everything he did, including his losses. When his forces fell at Gettysburg, he personally rode out to meet the survivors and told them, "It's all my fault. I thought my men were invincible." He said this in spite of the fact that, during the battle, some of his senior officers contributed to defeat by disobeying his orders. Lee didn't blame anyone, and he willingly accepted even the burden of defeat. His acceptance of complete responsibility made people revere him. Soldiers actually reached out to touch him when he passed by, as if encountering a holy person.

The *Star Trek* captains routinely do the same thing, accepting the full burden for problems and mistakes. When an enemy ship attacks the *Enterprise*, Kirk and Picard man the helm; when serious danger looms, they guide the away team; when the *Enterprise* gets into trouble, they answer to Starfleet. In the first episode of *Voyager*, Captain Janeway decides to destroy her ship's only way home in order to save the Ocampa planet. She strands her crewmembers seventy-five light-years away from the nearest starbase, leaving them frightened and angry. It doesn't help that many of them are political prisoners whom she's returning to stand trial. Even so, she manages to foster cooperation and trust. Instead of blaming the enemy or fate or anything else, Janeway takes full responsibility for her actions, promising the crew that she'll find them a way back home . . . somehow. What courage it takes to shoulder the distress and rage of an entire ship of marooned people! Although she may never see her loved ones again, Janeway spares herself no time to wallow in her own anguish.

Leaders always bear the heaviest burden, and they do so willingly. Attend any meeting and watch as the participants eagerly contribute their two cents—until it's time to delegate tasks. Then everybody suddenly looks down at their navels or stares out the window, as the natural Leader signs up for one thing after another. Why do the other group members become so reticent? Not out of laziness. They simply fear taking ultimate responsibility. They don't want to fail, thinking they'll get into trouble or lose a promotion if they screw up.

By contrast, Leaders are willing to take chances, even if it means making mistakes in the process. As the saying goes, nothing ventured, nothing gained. In *Smash the Pyramid*, authors William Doyle and William Perkins interviewed America's fastest-rising executives to discover the secrets of their success. The thirty-eight-year-old CEO of a biotechnology company told how he made it: "I would take the [lousiest] jobs that were available . . . in areas where other managers wouldn't go . . . I figured . . . that I can't do any worse here, and I have an opportunity to do very well. . . . You have to look at the fact that it's already a disaster, and that all you can do is make it better."

Picard would certainly agree. In the episode "Tapestry," Q gives him a chance to correct the errors of his wild and reckless youth. Picard happily obliges, rewriting his early life in a more mature, responsible key. But when Q shows him how his revised life-scenario plays out, Picard realizes that if he had played it safe all his life, he would have become a stodgy, boring person stuck in a menial position—instead of a starship Captain. He learns that the wild chances he took and the outlandish mistakes he made early in life allowed him to grow in strength and wisdom, and actually won him the notice of others. The lesson applies to all of us. If we don't take chances, we can't grow into leadership.

If only our politicians had Q to goose them! In the 1992 presidential election, no Democratic candidate dared to declare candidacy against George Bush, who rose in the popularity polls after the Gulf War. They feared that the Republican hold on the White House couldn't be shaken. Only when the polls showed that Bush was vulnerable because of his weak domestic record did candidates begin to throw hats into the ring. Unlike these tentative candidates, true Leaders make up their minds quickly, never waiting for risk-free conditions. As Victor Kiam, former owner of the Remington shaver company, said, "There is no greater failure than maybe."

General George Meade failed to make up his mind about what to do after winning the Battle of Gettysburg—pursue the rebel troops, or wait to fight another day. While he deliberated, Lee swiftly led the battered Confederates back across the Potomac to safety. Military historians agree that if Meade had acted quickly, he could have won the Civil War that day. Instead, the war dragged on for another two years, incurring tens of thousands more casualties.

General Meade wasn't the only procrastinator messing things up during the Civil War: General George McClellan was even worse. In 1862, Lincoln asked him to confront the Rebels at Manassas, Virginia, but McClellan wavered and finally defied Lincoln's battle plans. Instead, he advanced to Richmond, failed to seize the city, and then at last went to Manassas. Unfortunately, he arrived too late to be of any use. Lincoln was so frustrated by the general's inept leadership that he remarked dryly, "It is called the Army of the Potomac but it is only McClellan's bodyguard. If McClellan is not using the army, I should like to borrow it for a while." Vain, contemptuous of authority, and reluctant to do battle, McClellan was the epitome of a leader who refused to move decisively or seize opportunity when it stared him in the face.

Wes Roberts (in *Attila*) rates decisiveness high on the list of leadership qualities. Leaders actually *like* making life-and-death choices. Watch how quickly the *Star Trek* captains execute decisions in times of crisis. No gnashing of teeth, no labored weighing of alternatives. They clearly see the best course of action and go for it. In "If Wishes Were Horses," storybook characters invade *Deep Space Nine*. "Rumpelstiltskin" steals O'Brien's daughter, but when O'Brien manages to take his kid back, the imp gets angry and creates a space disturbance that will wipe out the entire station within thirty seconds. Rumpelstiltskin won't undo the disturbance unless Sisko hands the child back over. Faced with such a choice—destroy a young child or risk death— most of us would equivocate, but not Sisko. Without hesitation, he refuses the imp's demands and makes a few of his own. Fortunately, the anomaly turns out to be an illusion, the imp an alien, and nobody gets hurt in the end, but only because Sisko acted quickly enough.

The quality of decisiveness alone can catapult an unlikely person into a leadership position. Harry Truman didn't seem like presidential material to most observers when he took over the White House after F.D.R.'s death. The *New York Times* described him as being "without knowledge, without prestige." Winston Churchill said to him, "I must confess, Sir, I held you in very low regard." Truman appeared so ordinary, so undistinguished, and yet he's now recognized as one of the greatest presidents. Why? Because he had "the ability to decide . . . he never hesitated in the face of great decisions," said his friend, Jean Monnet, architect of the Common Market. Unlike many of his successors, Truman didn't twiddle his thumbs waiting for the results of the latest public opinion polls before taking action. Swiftly, unflinchingly, he decided to drop the bomb on Japan, to fire General MacArthur, to intervene in South Korea.

Truman wrote, "If you can't take the heat, get out of the

kitchen." He made decisions easily because he was prepared to accept the consequences of his actions, to "take the heat." And in fact, he took lots of heat, got lots of bad press, but never switched positions to mollify the public, never tried to whitewash his views. He said, "I became quite used to being vilified. It has its stimulating aspects, and for all I know, may even be good for the liver."

Who but a great Leader could find something positive even in the experience of public denunciation? Like Truman, the best Leaders remain cheerful and optimistic no matter what. If John Lennon had given up when his best friend Stu Sutcliff left the band, the Beatles never would have happened. If Anwar Sadat had gotten depressed when the Arab nations turned against him for initiating peace talks in the Middle East, he never would have forged a treaty with Israel. If the great composer Richard Wagner had changed careers after critics panned his operas, he wouldn't have written his master-piece, *The Ring Cycle*. And if Kirk had despaired in "The Changeling" when Nomad threatened to destroy all imperfect life forms, the entity would have wiped out "biological infestation" (including humanity) throughout the universe.

Even when things appear hopeless, Leaders keep the faith and remain devoted to their cause. As a young minister, years before his rise to prominence, Martin Luther King, Jr., vowed to dedicate himself to the fight for social justice. Years later, when he said "I have a dream . . ." he said it with such power and conviction that he enlisted millions of people to fight with him to turn that dream into reality. Dr. King's urgent belief in his mission consumed his entire life. You could see it in his eyes, hear it in his voice; today, you can feel it as you read about his life.

Although many people believe in some cause or other, very few *burn* with devotion to their cause. Leaders do, and their intensity lights the way for others to follow. How else could someone like Mahatma Gandhi, a rather simple and unimpressive man in his early days, inspire the support of millions of people? How else could Anne Hutchison—a woman living in the 1630s, when women were virtually powerless—lead a band of followers to Rhode Island to set up a new colony, even after she was tried for heresy for her radical view of the church? These Leaders, and so many others like them, inspire followers because their own blazing commitment to their ideals ignites a fire that spreads to their contemporaries.

The *Star Trek* captains certainly possess a consuming passion for their chosen missions. Their subordinates manage to have personal lives—Deanna and Riker have each other, Worf has his son, Kira has Vedek Bareil, Spock has his "music," Data has Spot—but as a rule the captains must forgo such luxuries. We get a glimpse of the personal price they pay for their dedication in various episodes. In the movie *Generations*, Kirk finally gets a chance to settle down with a woman he loves and actually seems blissfully happy, until Picard convinces him to give it all up. In "The Inner Light," an alien probe knocks out Picard and gives him a home life. Years later, in "Lessons," he reveals how profoundly dear that experience was to him. And Janeway, hurled light-years away from her family, comments that she wishes the ship had a counselor. Shortly after, she asks Chakotay, her first officer, to help her find her animal guide, but her spiritual quest is interrupted by ship's business. Like the other Starfleet captains, Janeway rarely gets a moment's rest.

Of course, command hasn't stopped most real life Leaders from enjoying romance. Even so, great Leaders often pay dearly for their all-encompassing devotion to their cause—either too little time with family, or no privacy or exhaustion and illness from working too hard. In the worst cases, they live with constant public disapproval or even become the targets of assassins. Lincoln comes to mind here. He endured the deaths of two of his sons and the enormous pressures of steering the Union he cherished through one of the bloodiest wars in history, all the while suffering a constant stream of invective from the press and his political opponents. Nor did he have any time to savor his achievements; he was assassinated just five days after the Civil War ended.

Leaders willingly endure such stresses because their vision of the future guides them onward. The rest of us may have an inkling of what we hope will happen in the world, but we don't spend our days creating a grand plan to make it so. Leaders do. In his "I have a dream" speech, King revealed his beautiful vision for the future of America. The founders of the United States expressed their vision in the Bill of Rights. John F. Kennedy had a vision of America: "Ask not what your country can do for you; ask what you can do for your country." Mikhail Gorbachev had a vision of a democratic Soviet Union, one that would undo much of the terror and hardship the people suffered for decades under a parade of dictators and despots. These Leaders all had an ideological headstart on the masses: Their visions spurred political, cultural, and social revolutions. And so leading—going first—ultimately means paving the way ideologically, to introduce bold new dreams, not just to walk in front of the troops.

Although they pursue their goals fervently, Leaders always find the time to encourage and defend their followers. So often, the *Star Trek* captains put themselves on the line to stand up for crew members. Picard acts as Worf's defender, or cha'Dich, risking his own life and his reputation in "Sins of the Father." Kirk disobeys a direct order from Starfleet and risks *his* career in order to take Spock to Vulcan to complete a mating ritual in "Amok Time." Then, he agrees to fight a no-win battle with Spock to let him complete the ritual, nearly getting himself killed. And Sisko insists on defending Dax when she gets accused of treason and murder, though evidence clearly points to her guilt.

To protect and defend their followers, numerous real-life Leaders have had to endure even the humiliation and anguish of accepting defeat. After the Battle of Bear Paw Mountains in 1877, Chief Joseph of the Nez Perce tribe laid down his spear. In an eloquent and tragic speech, he said, "Our chiefs are killed. . . . The old men are all dead. . . . The little children are freezing to death. My people, some of them have run away to the hills and have no blankets, no food. Hear me, my chiefs. My heart is sick and sad.

From where the sun now stands I will fight no more forever." The greatness of Chief Joseph's surrender can be found in his willingness to end his people's suffering, despite the anguish it caused him as their leader.

Great Leaders will do *anything* for their followers because they believe in them. They feel that without their followers, they have nothing, and so sacrifice continually for them, as parents do for children. They see strength and capacity in their subordinates when nobody else does, and this quality more than any other wins them undying loyalty and adoration.

Mary Kay Ash, head of the Mary Kay Cosmetics empire, started out with zilch sales ability. She tried to support three children by selling Stanley Home Products, but did so poorly that she could barely pay for her inventory—until she attended a sales convention. There, she watched as the top saleswoman of the year got crowned "queen." Something stirred in Mary Kay; though she was making only seven dollars a week at that time, she resolved to become queen the next year. She decided to tell somebody, so she tracked down the company president and boldly declared her intention to take the title of queen. Instead of laughing at her, he took her hand, looked her straight in the eye, and said, "You know, somehow I think you will." Mary Kay insists that "those seven words changed my life. I couldn't let him down."

Numerous management studies show that people perform best when they have supervisors who value them. "When you're constantly letting people know in some way that you know they're going to do the right thing and do great, and when you let them do it, they often do," says the president of an international hotel and resort chain.

The movie *Stand and Deliver*, based on a true story, shows the amazing effects of believing in people. A teacher in the Los Angeles school system in the 1970s takes over a class of supposedly stupid high school students who can barely add; some still use their fingers to count. The students bounce off the walls, completely undisciplined and unmotivated, but unlike other teachers, this one doesn't assign remedial work or detention. Instead, he tells the kids that they can achieve anything they want and that he intends to teach them calculus. The stretch seems ridiculous, but he persists, telling the kids, "You are the best, you are our hope for the future; remember that." He finally gets the kids to believe in themselves, startling authorities when 80 percent of his students pass advanced placement tests in calculus—tests that only 2 percent of American students have the guts even to try.

To those students, Jaime Escalante—their teacher—became the greatest person on earth. True Leaders never gain their authority by lording it over others. Instead, they win trust—even reverence—by encouraging and inspiring people.

At the beginning of *Voyager*, Paris has no self-respect. He has a criminal record, and in fact comes aboard *Voyager* as a political prisoner to guide the ship to the hiding place of guerrilla rebels. He beats on himself for a host of errors made early in his career. In spite of his defeated, almost hostile manner, Janeway sees something special in him, and to his utter astonishment, she makes him her pilot. Of course, he rises to the occasion beautifully. When she does the same thing for the belligerent B'Elanna Torres, naming her Chief Engineer, the entire crew takes note. By showing respect and loyalty to her rag-tag crew of dissidents, Janeway quickly earns loyalty, cooperation, and respect in return.

Picard, too, knows this secret. When Data, an android, goes on trial to determine whether he should be dismantled, Picard fights tooth and nail for him, insisting that Data has a soul, has viability, and must be treated with respect. He goes to bat for Data a second time when Data creates a "child," which Starfleet wants to take away from him. Picard's belief in Data pays off in the final episode; as others accuse the captain of senility, Data stands loyally by his side.

All the *Star Trek* captains provide exemplary models of leadership. Kirk has a bit more feistiness than the others, Picard a bit more of the wise king, and Janeway a bit more of the nurturer, but all possess impeccable integrity, remarkable courage, more expertise and cunning than anyone else on board, sterling self-confidence, constant kindness, clear vision, and unshakable faith in their crew members. What else could you possibly want in a boss? If only the real world served up Leaders like Kirk, Picard, Sisko, and Janeway a bit more often. To work under any one of them would be an unforgettable, cherished experience, an honor and a privilege. The only thing better would be to become like them yourself, and that's exactly what this section of the book will help you to do.

In the all-time favorite *Star Trek* episode, "The City on the Edge of Forever," Kirk goes back in time to the 1930s and falls deeply in love with a social worker named Edith Keeler. Unlike most of Kirk's romances, this one isn't a mere flirtation; he's head over heels. Meanwhile, Spock reviews newsreels from a few days into the future and discovers that Edith will soon get hit by a car and die. He also discovers that if Kirk tries to save her, she'll live to start a peace movement that will inadvertently allow the Nazis to win World War II. Knowing this, Kirk must stand by as Edith walks out in front of the car that kills her. Although everything in him wants to stop her, he can't. His commitment to preserve the future of humanity forces him to let the woman he loves die.

Although Leaders certainly have the capacity to love deeply, their mission always comes first. Like Kirk, they'll sacrifice their loved ones if need be. The spouses of Leaders often live tortured existences, spending too much time alone while their mates travel, lead rallies, or simply cogitate on more important matters. That might be tolerable if only the Leader-partner was faithful, but alas, Leaders too often have wandering eyes.

Strong Leaders attract the opposite sex the way ice cream sundaes attract hungry kids: As Henry Kissinger said, "Power is the ultimate aphrodisiac." Women drop dead for Kirk and Picard.

Around every powerful Leader, a coterie of amorous hopefuls gather, heaping praise and adoration upon them. Combine that with the constant travel and intense pressure that Leaders live with, and you can see why they so often yield to temptation. Too many nights away from home, too many problems, too many beautiful people willing to offer comfort and fun.

Even our greatest Leaders have lousy track records in the faithful spouse department. J.F.K. messed around, his brothers messed around, F.D.R. messed around, Martin Luther King had affairs, John Lennon cheated on Yoko, and so on. It takes a special partner to put up with the Leader's wanderings. Of course, not all Leaders let their libido get out of hand. Mikhail Gorbachev, Harry Truman, and George Washington all had spotless records—good "family values"—but their spouses still had to deal with very distracted mates.

It seems that when a Leader *does* find the right partner—someone strong in his or her own right, who completely identifies with the Leader's mission—a mighty and enduring bond can be forged. Harry Truman's letters to his wife Bess show a depth of commitment so rare that one fights back tears reading them. Farther back in history, Napoleon and Josephine enjoyed a passionate romance, fueled in no small measure by her attraction to a powerful conqueror. When Kirk finally does fall in love with Edith Keeler, it's the real thing, his passion practically jumping off the screen. Same thing with Picard, when he falls for a stellar cartographer in "Lessons." He's so smitten that it's hard to watch. And Sisko never really recovers from the death of his one true love, his wife.

Here's some advice for anyone seeking a relationship with a Leader: Make sure you have a life of your own. Or at least, be certain that you share your partner's passion for the mission. At best, you can hang on for the ride of your life, getting swept into a whirlwind of activity around something that truly excites you while sharing love with a person whom you respect down to your very bones. At worst, you'll play second fiddle to a big shot, neglected and forgotten in the dust of more pressing matters.

Just as a plant needs sunlight and water, Leaders blossom when allowed to exercise both responsibility and authority. If they don't have that power, they become rebellious and ornery. Usually, though, they rise to the top in their organizations, gaining recognition quickly by their willingness to do dirty jobs that nobody else will tackle, by their integrity, their generosity and concern for others, their exceptional talents, their physical stamina and unusual vitality. Leaders also tend to make noise that gets them noticed, never letting their own accomplishments (or anyone else's) go unsung.

Although they want to hold the reins, true Leaders won't knock you down to grab them. Leaders are team players; they proceed with dignity and integrity in all matters. In fact, they'll do everything possible to help you advance, never fearing competition. That's how Leaders win friends throughout the organization; that's why everybody cheers when they rise up the ladder.

In episode after episode, Picard does everything possible to cultivate his people. He encourages Riker to take a promotion to a captain's post; he gives Data a shot at command, he even makes Wesley an ensign. As he grooms his people for growth, they become ever more grateful to him and work hard to justify his faith in them. In fact, they become so loyal and grateful that they don't want to leave his side, as Riker demonstrates when he refuses several promotions so he can continue to serve with Jean-Luc. The lesson Picard teaches us is that if you do everything possible to help people find their own wings so that they can soar beyond you, they'll probably perch on your shoulder and serve you devotedly instead.

And so, to become a hero-Leader, you must develop a burning passion for something you believe in, and let that passion consume everything you think and do. Then you must cultivate a clear vision of where that passion can lead, and boldly share your vision with others. You must make choices without equivocating—and you must treat people as if you need them and respect them wholeheartedly. If you do these things, you won't need to seek out leadership roles; you will rise into leadership effortlessly, the way a feather floats to the surface of water.

QUICK LEADER PROFILE

A LEADER'S FAVORITE MOVIES:
Twelve Angry Men; Stand and Deliver; Dead Poets Society; Mr. Smith Goes to Washington; Henry V; Cry Freedom; Gandhi; Braveheart; A Few Good Men

A LEADER'S FAVORITE BOOKS:
The Prince, by Machiavelli; *How to Win Friends and Influence People,* by Dale Carnegie; *The One-Minute Manager,* by Kenneth H. Blanchard and Spencer Johnson; *Leadership Secrets of Attila the Hun,* by Wes Roberts; *Fail Safe,* by Eugene Burdick and Harvey Wheeler; *Seven Habits of Highly Effective People,* by Stephen R. Covey

A LEADER'S IDEA OF A GREAT VACATION:
Charter your own boat; tour the White House; go to Camp David or Monticello

THE LEADER'S MOTTO:
"Follow me."

GOOD JOBS FOR LEADERS:
CEO; school principal; department manager; coach; military commander; hospital director; chief administrator; pope; mayor; governor; king

WHAT YOU'LL FIND IN A LEADER'S OFFICE:
Pictures of world rulers on the wall; honors and awards on shelves; a white board with organizational charts hanging somewhere; motivational sayings on the desk; a secretary in the corner trying to organize piles of paper

A LEADER'S WORST NIGHTMARES:

Becoming a secretary; having jury duty and not being foreman; being called "cute"

FAMOUS LEADERS:

George Washington; Mary Kay Ash; Harriet Tubman; Harry Truman; Franklin Delano Roosevelt; Anwar Sadat; Mikhail Gorbachev; Martin Luther King; Robin Hood; Mahatma Gandhi; Winston Churchill; John Lennon; Coach Pat Riley

14

A LITTLE PICARD GETS YOU UP

OFF THE COUCH (BUT TOO MUCH

MAKES YOU RIPE FOR A COUP)

When in charge, ponder. When in trouble, delegate. When in doubt, mumble.

—Good Life Almanac

In the classic episode "Who Mourns for Adonais?" Kirk and crew get kidnapped by the Greek god Apollo, who plunks them down on an asteroid in the middle of nowhere and then insists that they worship him. By exercising his supernatural muscle, Apollo creates havoc: A female crew member goes gaga for him, Scotty gets jealous of him, and McCoy becomes paralyzed with worry. Thank goodness for Kirk's leadership. He thinks of only one thing: how to get back to the ship. He orders Scotty to focus on escaping and quit the histrionics, commands the smitten female crewmember to give Apollo the shaft, and demands that McCoy galvanize his resources and exhaust Apollo by provoking him. The crew outwits Apollo in the end—but only because of Kirk's single-minded focus.

Although you'll probably never get marooned on an asteroid with a jealous god, you can easily land in serious trouble if you don't know where you want to go in life. Kirk shows how having a sense of mission can save your skin, can keep you from getting lost, distracted, even killed.

How many of us get stuck in ruts because we have no vision of what we want from life, no burning sense of purpose? We endure jobs that don't thrill us, relationships that don't fulfill us, we feel strung-out and uptight and a million miles from the ideals of our youth. We have no ultimate goal to guide the choices that we make in life, no compelling dreams that we strive to realize. And so, we mechanically go through the motions of living, hoping that inspiration will someday dawn on its own.

"The difference between a rut and a grave is the depth," said Bishop Gerald Burrill. In other words, without a strong sense of purpose, we live life with one foot already in the grave. Even knowing this, we don't take time to think about our life goals. Who has the time to ponder such things, with all the pressures of modern life constantly weighing us down—bills to pay, meetings to attend, and projects to bring home?

Leaders do. Leaders make it their business to think about what they want out of life, and to keep their life-purpose constantly before them. They don't wait until vacation to ponder "the meaning of it all." Their life-goal gets them through the days until vacation; it burns inside them each minute.

Do you really know what you want out of life? Do you have long-term life goals? If not, you need to invoke your inner Picard pronto. Observe how Picard knows exactly what he wants at all times. Temptations constantly bombard him—opportunities for romance, other job offers, extended vacations on blissful planets—but he never takes the bait. He never violates the Prime Directive, either, though so often it would make his job easier. Instead, he gives everything he's got to his chosen mission—to command the starship *Enterprise* and peaceably explore the galaxy. That's what makes him a great Captain.

Martin Luther King, Jr., once said, "If a man hasn't discovered something that he will die for, then he isn't fit to live." Dr. King may have had a rather radical view, but he *did* have a point. You do need to have passion for *something*—or depression inevitably comes. That's what happens in the mid-life crisis. You suddenly realize that you don't have dreams anymore, that you mechanically go through day after day without achieving anything, without becoming anything, while time keeps slipping by.

Of course, you don't need to be forty-something to suffer from a lack of life-direction. Wesley Crusher goes into a tailspin when he loses interest in his studies at Starfleet Academy in the episode "Journey's End." He mopes around the ship feeling blue, snapping at people, having no idea what to do with his life. His suffering ends only when a character called the Traveler befriends him and shows him how to find his true direction.

Like Wesley, many of us have trouble pursuing (or even recognizing) our own passions because people expect us to take a traditional path and we listen too much to their advice; or because we have talent in an area that doesn't really interest us but we think it makes sense to pursue it; or we can't bear to risk failure in an area that does excite us. But as Wesley discovered, we won't find lasting happiness unless we dedicate ourselves to something we care deeply about.

What if nothing excites you, if you feel no enduring sense of mission? How do you light a fire under yourself? As always, *Star Trek* provides some clues. With help from the Traveler, Wesley goes on a vision quest to explore his dreams. In "Rightful Heir," Worf embarks on a prolonged spiritual retreat when he feels empty and lost. Janeway asks Chakotay to help her identify her animal guide. You need to do something similar, to take dedicated time and space to think about what you want from life. You can't wait around hoping that God will leave a message on your answering machine revealing your life's mission to you. Answers don't drop from the sky. You must make a concerted effort to know your own dreams, to find your special path—and you must make this undertaking your first priority. If need be, see a counselor. Read self-help books. Go on a vision quest. Write about your dreams, your goals. And do the Leader exercises in the next chapter.

Fortunately, most of us already have some notion of what we want from life, but it's incredibly difficult to stay focused on that goal from minute to minute. We might be reminded of the goal during times of heightened awareness—during a funeral or a wedding, for example, or when we manage to carve out a moment to engage in quiet contemplation. But in our daily life, we worry only about the details of doing business as usual. Our preoccupied minute-life opens the wormhole to self-annihilation, where we lose ourselves and our dreams in worry and petty concerns.

To the greatest extent possible, you must make your life's mission an integral part of every breath you take. Everything you do—every job you accept, every person you befriend, every penny you spend—should support your mission. Otherwise, you won't achieve your dream. Focusing imparts power. The diffuse rays of a flashlight barely light up the road ten feet ahead. But when those rays cohere into a single laser beam, they become not just bright but powerful enough to penetrate steel. In the same way, when you gather your life-energy around a single goal, you gain tremendous strength.

Every great accomplishment in history resulted from somebody's intense focus. Thomas Edison developed 3,000 failed theories before he got the lightbulb to work. He also unsuccessfully tested filaments from 6,000 distinct species of plants, tried out materials from 1,600 minerals, and wrote 40,000 pages of laboratory notes in 200 different notebooks. No wonder he said "genius is one percent inspiration and ninety-nine percent perspiration." Alex Haley spent twenty years trying to find a publisher for his massive novel *Roots* before he finally found a buyer. And Abraham Lincoln failed in business twice and unsuccessfully ran for office three times before he won the Presidency. Yet all of these people eventually succeeded because they concentrated their energy around a singular purpose.

If you have no desire to invent lightbulbs or publish a great book or do anything else earth-shattering, fine. But don't think that lets you off the hook. To achieve self-fulfillment, you must discover a focus in your life. Even if your goals are modest, you need to make a concerted, constant effort to achieve them. Take a lesson from Quark. In "If Wishes Were Horses," he gets so distracted by some beautiful women that he doesn't even notice when his customers rob him blind. Quark has a life-goal: to get rich and acquire as much property as possible. Hardly noble, but at least it's a goal. Still, he constantly gets sidetracked, so he's stuck doing grunt work at the *Deep Space Nine* bar. We all make the same mistakes as Quark, and often on a much grander scale. We want a rich family life, but get sidetracked by demands at work and spend too much time away from home. We want a fulfilling spiritual life, but watch television instead of praying or meditating. We want to lose weight but won't give up desserts until *after* Thanksgiving. By failing to focus intensely enough on what we really want, we end up frustrated and unsuccessful at best; at worst, we find ourselves in real trouble.

Look at what happened to the emperor Nero because he fiddled around instead of ruling Rome. He spent his time writing poetry, racing chariots, giving public performances on the lyre—everything but conducting affairs of state. His subjects lost faith in him, burned Rome to the ground, and finally overthrew the government while he studied art in Greece. Ultimately, declared a public enemy by the senate, he killed himself. He lost everything because he had no sense of mission, no focus.

In contrast, Kirk's sense of mission lets him constantly make hard choices without any hair-pulling whatsoever. In "Arena," he gets forced to fight a Gorn—a huge lizardlike alien—to the death. Kirk defeats the Gorn, but at the last minute decides not to kill him, in spite of everybody's expectations that he will. Even in the heat of battle, Kirk manages to stay focused on his mission: to explore life in the galaxy, not destroy it.

And so, you need to identify your life's mission and then focus wholeheartedly on it. Having a firm grasp on your life's purpose will help you to make sound decisions. We become indecisive and get into trouble when we have no abiding value system, no context, no Prime Directive to guide us in making choices.

If any of the *Star Trek* captains couldn't instantly make up their minds about what to do when enemy ships uncloaked before them, they'd end up space dust in nanoseconds. They'd also spend more time in sick bay, suffering from migraines, anxiety, insomnia. Indecision takes a real toll on the body and the psyche. As Bertrand Russell said, "Nothing is so exhausting as indecision, and nothing is so futile."

Shakespeare's *Hamlet* provides a classic example of the problems engendered by indecision. Hamlet can't decide what to do after his uncle kills his dad, even after his father's ghost visits him and tells him to avenge the murder. While he procrastinates and debates with himself over life-and-death questions ("To be, or not to be . . ."), he accidentally kills his tutor, his lover goes insane, he kills his cousin in a sword fight, and in the end, goes wacky and kills himself. Oh, what a noble mind is here o'erthrown—and all because, alas, he kneweth not how to bestir his inner Picard.

Like Hamlet, many of us resist grabbing the mantle of leadership. We want to let somebody else call the shots because we don't want to carry the weighty burden of responsibility, or we believe that we have no leadership qualities anyway, and so happily hover in the background doing support work. We might even congratulate ourselves on our humility, our lack of competitive ego—"I don't need to be a big-shot leader." Too often, such an attitude actually covers up for laziness, unwillingness, and fear.

If you routinely look to others to take the reins, you need a good kick. You have a Leader within (and so does everybody else), and at least one area where you excel and can assume a principal role. Why bother? Because other people can't benefit from your talents and wisdom if you hide out doing only the menial. By always taking a back seat, you may save yourself some problems, but you also fail to develop your own potential or to make a significant contribution, and you fail to help others develop their potential. More than anything else, leadership means cultivating others, seeing their strengths and helping bring them forward. When you develop the talents of others and help them to manifest their good qualities, you offer the greatest of gifts.

This doesn't mean that you should jump up right now and run for the state senate. It only implies that once in a while, in some small area of your life, you should put yourself on the line and stop depending on others to take the lead. Growing up has its downside, but the upside is that you no longer have to take orders from adults. You now have the capacity to take charge of things yourself, just by virtue of being a big person.

If you don't have any special expertise that qualifies you to take charge, develop it. In *The Art of the Leader*, author William A. Cohen writes, "If you want people . . . to seek you out as their unofficial leader, all you need to do is develop a needed expertise. . . . You can become an expert in just about anything in five years or less. There is only one requirement. You must put forth the effort." To make his case, Cohen discusses a couple of guys named Steve Jobs and Stephen Wozniak. After they dropped out of high school, they spent a mere five years learning about computers. Then they launched their company and gave it a juicy name: Apple.

In the *Next Generation* episode "Hollow Pursuits," the meek officer Barclay spends his time hiding out in the holodeck, living in a fantasy world where he imagines himself to be a great hero. Back in reality, though, he kowtows to everybody, believes he has no special talents. He certainly wouldn't dream of taking charge of anything at all. But when a malfunction threatens to destroy the *Enterprise* within minutes, Barclay is the one who fixes the problem—to his own surprise, as well as to everybody else's. The episode shows that when pushed, the most unassuming and subservient of people can take the reins and accomplish great things. It also shows how much we fail to develop our capacities when we keep ourselves always in the background.

Many movies and books portray people who never showed leadership potential before suddenly filling big boots. In the film *Dave*, a regular guy who happens to look like the president gets kidnapped and asked to fill in for the dying head-of-state. His captors want him to make a few public appearances without saying anything or doing anything presidential—just wave from the limo window and then disappear. But Dave unexpectedly decides to take advantage of his executive office. To the horror of his captors, he shoots off his mouth, makes executive decisions, and turns out to be a great president. Likewise, in the movie *Big*, a kid gets his wish and grows up suddenly, though he still has the brain of a ten-year-old. Even so, he manages to become head of marketing of an international toy company, and does quite well in the post.

Buckminster Fuller said, "Everyone is born a genius, but the process of living de-geniuses them." Carrying the thought one step further, we are all born Leaders, but accumulated fear and self-doubt and lethargy often turn us into sheep. To boldly live, you need to wake up your "leadership lion" and reclaim your inner Picard. You can definitely do it. The exercises in the next chapter will get you started.

If somebody called you "bossy," how would you feel? Terrible, right? Few qualities carry such negative connotations. Having too little Leader can make you useless, but having too much can make you obnoxious, even dangerous.

Most of us carry the mantle of power clumsily. We tend to go overboard when we get into a Leadership role—overcontrolling, overmonitoring, overreacting. Why? Because we get overwhelmed by the demands of leadership. We find it incredibly stressful to keep track of so many issues, make so many decisions, coordinate so many people. To stay on top of it all, we try to control every little detail. We worry that our subordinates won't do a good enough job, so we ride them every minute. Terrified that they'll forget to do something important, we nitpick them to death. Fearing that we'll be held accountable if something goes wrong, we sit on top of people and prevent them from doing anything.

To lead well takes a great deal of self-acceptance, confidence, integrity, and compassion. You can't try to control what others think or do, you can't believe you're better than those you lead, and you can't feel threatened when people criticize you. Unfortunately, most people in leadership roles don't have these special qualities; as a result, leadership problems riddle almost every organization on Earth. The bad Leader problem is so pervasive that entire industries (organizational development, industrial psychology, management consulting) have been created to help people become better leaders.

In spite of all the books and workshops and consultants available to help, rotten Leaders still abound. You can't survive adulthood without knowing at least one overly bossy boss, one person who tries to shove a mission down your throat, one chief who assumes all control singlehandedly—failing to delegate appropriately, failing to listen to anybody else's input.

Star Trek certainly has its share of overzealous officers. In the *Next Generation* episode "The Pegasus," Riker gets assigned to work with Admiral Pressman, with whom he had served many years ago. Their starship, *Pegasus*, which supposedly blew up, now mysteriously reappears, lodged inside of an asteroid. Pressman wants to recover sensitive equipment from the ship, and he'll do anything to get it back. He doesn't care what the rest of the crew thinks or wants: He yells at them to carry out his orders, commands them to make risky maneuvers, makes all the decisions himself, and even disregards Picard's recommendations. Picard finally discovers that the *Pegasus* crew mutinied because of Pressman's obsessive command style and the questionable nature of his mission. Ironically, the *Enterprise* crew does the same thing, turning the helm back over to Picard, placing Pressman under arrest.

If you refuse to delegate or to collaborate, you inevitably foster resentment among your subordinates. In real life, Admiral Pressman's sad story replays in countless settings, always with the same ending: the demise of the autocratic leader. The E. F. Hutton story provides a case in point. In 1970, Robert Foman became the CEO of the E. F. Hutton empire. When he first assumed control, annual revenues were at $1.1 billion, but by 1985, the firm dissolved in a takeover by Shearson-American Express. What went wrong? According to an article in *Fortune,* Foman acted like a feudal lord. He hired and promoted anybody he felt like rewarding, including, not surprisingly, his close friends. He made it his business to review personally the salaries and bonuses of more than a thousand employees. Imagine Bill Clinton poring over the account ledgers to see how much the treasury pays the person who cleans dishes in a Smithsonian cafeteria! According to *Fortune,* Foman's whole life was devoted to "holding court, making all the large and small decisions."

As Foman discovered too late, you can't run an organization singlehandedly. This truth applies to all organizations, from major conglomerates down to the family unit. If you try to do everything by yourself, to make all the decisions, the people under you will feel left out and disregarded, and they'll rebel. Plus, you'll inevitably make serious mistakes. True Leaders realize that they need a team behind them; they believe in the wisdom of the checks-and-balances system.

Sometimes people hog all the power for themselves because they become overly obsessed with their mission. Their fixation on achieving their goals makes them frantic. They don't want to take the time to bring others aboard, or risk having others delay progress by challenging their views. True, having a life-mission is an important thing, but you also need to cultivate patience and perspective. You can't impose your mission on other people without serious consequences.

Captain Decker disregards this wisdom in the classic episode "The Doomsday Machine" after a giant object in space severely damages his ship and kills his entire crew. Gripped by guilt over his failure to save his crew, Decker becomes neurotically obsessed with the goal of destroying the deadly object at all costs. He transports to the *Enterprise* and snags control while Kirk and company try to repair his ship. He puts the *Enterprise* at great peril in his reckless chase maneuvers, disregards the crew's objections, and gets so carried away that he even refuses a direct order from Kirk to turn the helm back over to Spock. Finally, the crew forcibly removes him from duty.

Unfortunately, people like Decker abound in the real world, sometimes letting their obsessions bring about widespread destruction. Apocalyptic cult Leaders become totally obsessed with making preparations for the end of the world, and in some cases lead their followers right down the path to doom and destruction. James Jones of Jonestown made his adherents so completely dependent on him by denying them access to the outside world and even to their own families that they believed him when he told them the world was ending. Nine hundred of them simultaneously drank poison and killed themselves at his command. "Leadership does not depend on being right," said educator Ivan Illich, and so Jones proved.

In a similar but even more extreme case, Shoko Asahara of Japan recently ordered his followers to release nerve gas in a Tokyo subway as a practice run for the "coming end of the world," when they'll need to fight off the evil forces that will attack them. Despite subjecting followers to rigorous prolonged fasts and requiring them to turn over all their worldly possessions, he cultivated 40,000 disciples. After the event, police found that Asahara had enough chemicals stockpiled to kill 4.2 million people.

When Leaders impose their values on others, they always extract a price from their followers, even if they don't cause death and destruction. In the *Next Generation* episode "Birthright, Part II," Worf discovers Klingons living under Romulan rule on a distant planet. The Romulan leader has "domesticated" the Klingons and shaped them in his own image, not allowing them to retain their Klingon culture or customs. Although he appears benevolent and insists that the end justifies the means—he has achieved unprecedented peace between the two peoples—Worf disagrees, finding conditions on the planet unbearable and humiliating. Ultimately, the Klingons realize that Worf has a point: They feel spiritually dead from denying their heritage for so long. They decide that they would rather die than continue following the Romulan Leader. This episode shows that you can't justify (or get away with) denying people freedom for too long. Ultimately, they'll rebel.

Even so, Leaders sometimes *do* accomplish significant things by ruling with an iron fist, and so convince themselves that they *must* act as they do. J. Edgar Hoover made the FBI a strong and central organization during his fifty years as Director, but he used vicious means to destroy people he disagreed with politically. Hoover justified his actions because, he said, he was fighting the "communist threat." He terrorized and discredited all people who dared to argue with him. For ammunition, he gathered dirt about their personal lives. He falsely accused his enemies of communist activities, manipulated crime data to support his theories, spied on foes of presidents whom he wanted to gain favor with, attacked civil rights leaders and those with liberal sentiments, and generally was known to have wielded more power, for a longer period, than any man in American history. Although Hoover enjoyed immense popularity in the early years of his regime, he fell into disfavor as his methods and hidden agenda came into public focus.

"Dictators are rulers who always look good until the last ten minutes," said Jan Masaryk, a politician. But the frightening thing is that even evil leaders, if they have one iota of charisma, have no problem finding followers *before* the last ten minutes. As the heroic Leader inspires people and gets the best out them, the diabolic Leader often gets the worst out of them. Such Leaders convince the masses that their warped mission has validity, and enlist thousands, even millions, to aid them in unleashing untold horrors. Mussolini made a religion out of fascism. Hitler went way beyond Mussolini, using the idea of Aryan supremacy to convince his followers that the end justifies the means. Stalin killed as many as 15 million peasants in a mere five-year period in order to rebuild the Soviet Union. Although he accomplished great things—enlarging the Soviet territory and making Russia the second most important industrial nation in the world—he also caused more deaths than anyone else before him and left his nation spiritually bereft.

"To persuade is more trouble than to dominate, and the powerful seldom take the trouble if they can avoid it," said American sociologist Charles Horton Cooley. The Leader unmodulated can become unthinkably diabolic. In "The Enemy Within," Spock says, "What is it that makes a man an exceptional leader? We see here that it is his negative side . . . properly controlled and disciplined [that] is vital to his strength." In other words, you need some aggressive energy in order to lead, but you need to *control and discipline* that energy. If you don't, you can easily go overboard and turn into a tyrant.

And what will help you to achieve the right balance between passion and obsession, between leadership and domination? How will you control the urge to act like a big cheese? For one thing, you must develop *all* of your inner heroes simultaneously and work to keep these different qualities in balance. Great Leaders, more than the other heroic types, display a blend of all the heroic qualities. You can't inspire confidence in people if you don't have a strong Relater, you can't make good decisions if you lack Analyst qualities, you can't act courageously if you don't have a ready Warrior.

The *Star Trek* captains all provide superb role models. Kirk has almost as much Warrior as Leader, Picard blends Analyst traits with his Leader qualities, Sisko has both Warrior and Analyst qualities, and Janeway has lots of Relater traits. In fact, the *Star Trek* captains have so many heroic qualities that you might think you could never become anything like them.

What would Picard say if he heard you express such doubts? He'd point out that you need to develop your Leader qualities, and order you to make it so! You *can* take charge of your life, achieve your dreams, and even inspire other people. Turn to the exercises in the next chapter for help.

15

Where I is, is where I is—but where I'm going is up to me.
—Charles J. Givens, Super Self

Okay career-hoppers, lost puppies, lazy bums: It's time to make your life count for something. No more drifting from interest to interest, accomplishing nothing. No more lost resolutions. No more endless nights of Oreos in front of the tube because "life stinks and then you die." You *can* still dream, you can realize your dreams—but you have to get off your duff and wake up your inner Picard right now. Time is passing! Carpe diem! The time is now.

You wouldn't admire Picard and Kirk and Sisko and Janeway if you didn't have a little bit of their spirit tucked deep inside of you. So practice the exercises on the next pages to wake up that spirit, and study the Leader Checklist that follows. Make a plan for your life, and boldly go where you never dreamed possible before.

LEADER CHECKLIST

- ❑ Stand tall and staight.
- ❑ Make the first move.
- ❑ Look people in the eye.
- ❑ Use controlled gestures.
- ❑ Dress for success.
- ❑ Move energetically.
- ❑ Project your voice.
- ❑ Speak with authority; don't mumble or hesitate.
- ❑ Get right to the point.
- ❑ Let enthusiasm radiate from you.

EXERCISE 1

Look Like a Leader

Practice this exercise in front of a mirror. Remember to watch *Star Trek* episodes for inspiration any time you need help in capturing the Leader "look."

1. **Warm up by watching *Star Trek* Leaders.** Good choices include Kirk in the classic episodes "The City on the Edge of Forever," "The Devil in the Dark," and "This Side of Paradise"; Picard in the *Next Generation* episodes "Chain of Command," "The Measure of a Man," and "Tapestry"; Sisko in *Deep Space Nine* episodes "Dax" and "Paradise"; and Janeway in the *Voyager* episode "Caretaker."

2. **Stand tall.** Have you ever seen a Leader who slouched? Leaders have exemplary posture. It's one of the things that sets them apart from others.

3. **Maintain direct eye contact,** but don't glare like a Warrior or flirt like a Relater. The Leader uses eye contact like a handshake: to open a channel for businesslike communications.

4. **Use controlled gestures to emphasize points.** Leaders express enthusiasm and energy for their vision through gestures,

but they don't flail wildly like Relaters. All their movements have a dignified control.

5. Dress for success. Leaders look smart. Would you want to follow someone who had shirttails sticking out, crumpled clothes, or ring-around-the collar? You must look fit to lead.

6. Extend yourself. Leaders take initiative. Don't wait for others to shake your hand: Approach people with your hand already extended. Practice making the first move.

7. Gather no moss. Leaders don't sit still for long. They often pace as they plan, walk as they talk, and jump up quickly whenever something needs to be done.

8. Stride with pride. Leaders show confidence even in their walk. They move with extraordinary energy.

EXERCISE 2

Talk Like a Leader

This exercise will help you to express yourself with a Leader's conviction and strength. If you mumble, stumble, or equivocate when you speak, you'll find this exercise particularly useful. Apply this exercise to different situations:

❑ asking for donations for your favorite cause
❑ volunteering to take charge of a project
❑ convincing a friend to help you paint your room
❑ discussing your desire for a promotion with your boss

1. Warm up by listening to Kirk, Picard, Sisko, and Janeway in any of your favorite episodes.

2. Pipe up. Studies show that leaders often have slightly louder voices than their peers, especially when they delegate tasks or try to make a point.

3.   Drop the "um." Leaders know what they want to say. They don't stumble around in their speech or use nervous expressions.

4.   Go deep. Leaders often have rich, deep voices. Avoid using shrill tones. Listen to Picard and Sisko, and see if you can emulate their tone.

5.   Put muscle in your mouth. Leaders speak with authority. Feel that you are injecting your words with power. *Never* mumble or look down as you talk. Don't let your sentences trail off at the end.

6.   Forget flowery prose. Leaders get right to the point in their speech. Don't beat around the bush, use overly colorful descriptions, or hesitate. Say what you mean.

7.   Get rhythm. Leaders know how to time what they say for greatest effect, pausing in the right places, emphasizing particular phrases and words. Listen to Picard's speech in "All Good Things…" Try varying your pace and volume as you speak to enhance the impact.

8.   Be enthusiastic. Leaders inspire others by projecting energy and enthusiasm. Speak with dynamism. Don't complain or let depression show in your communications.

EXERCISE 3

Identify Your Life's Mission

Leaders decide what they want, plan the steps that will lead to their success, and execute their plan. Follow the steps below to chart your journey to success.

1.   **Prioritize your values.** To identify your mission, you must first prioritize your values. Rank the list of values below in order of priority to you (highest value = 1, next highest value = 2, etc.). One way to do this is to imagine that you can only

have one of the values on this list. Which one would it be? Then imagine that you can have one more value. Continue this process until you have prioritized all the values on the list. Add your own values if they don't appear, and include them in the ranking process.

_____ financial success
_____ a loving relationship with my children
_____ good friends
_____ fun
_____ travel
_____ being self-employed
_____ physical security
_____ a fulfilled spiritual life
_____ a loving relationship with a significant other
_____ an excellent career
_____ accomplishment
_____ more free time
_____ lots of toys (boats, stereo systems, cars, etc.)
_____ a beautiful home
_____ a good boss
_____ being known as an expert in my field
_____ inner peace
_____ charity work
_____ contributing to the world
_____ creative activities (playing music, art, writing, etc.)

2. **List the top five values you identified, in priority order:**
   Under each value, indicate the amount of time you currently spend actively pursuing that value each month.

Value #1:_____

No time _____   1–2 hrs._____
3–5 hrs. _____   5–10 hrs._____
11–20 hrs._____   20+ hrs. _____

Value #2:_____

No time _____   1–2 hrs._____
3–5 hrs. _____   5–10 hrs._____
11–20 hrs._____   20+ hrs. _____

Value #3: _____

No time _____   1–2 hrs._____
3–5 hrs. _____   5–10 hrs._____
11–20 hrs._____   20+ hrs. _____

Value #4: _____

No time _____   1–2 hrs._____
3–5 hrs. _____   5–10 hrs._____
11–20 hrs._____   20+ hrs. _____

Value #5: _____

No time _____   1–2 hrs._____
3–5 hrs. _____   5–10 hrs._____
11–20 hrs._____   20+ hrs. _____

3.   **How much time do you actually want to spend on each of your top values in a month?** How much time would you need to achieve satisfaction?

Value #1: _____

No time _____   1–2 hrs._____
3–5 hrs. _____   5–10 hrs._____
11–20 hrs._____   20+ hrs. _____

Value #2: _____

No time _____   1–2 hrs._____
3–5 hrs. _____   5–10 hrs._____
11–20 hrs._____   20+ hrs. _____

Value #3: _____

No time _____	1–2 hrs. _____
3–5 hrs. _____	5–10 hrs. _____
11–20 hrs. _____	20+ hrs. _____

Value #4: _____

No time _____	1–2 hrs. _____
3–5 hrs. _____	5–10 hrs. _____
11–20 hrs. _____	20+ hrs. _____

Value #5: _____

No time _____	1–2 hrs. _____
3–5 hrs. _____	5–10 hrs. _____
11–20 hrs. _____	20+ hrs. _____

4. **Assess how you actually spend most of your time.** Are you spending as much time as you want or need to on your top values? If so, you don't need to continue with this exercise. You are well on the way to fulfilling your mission. Most people, though, will find a yawning chasm between what they value, and how they actually spend their time. Now take a look at what you spend most of your time doing: For each item below, write the number of hours each week you dedicate to that activity. Add anything that you spend significant time on to the list.

___ eating
___ sleeping
___ reading the newspaper
___ reading novels, mysteries, fun books
___ watching television/videos
___ talking on the telephone
___ shopping for food and necessities
___ shopping for fun
___ compulsive shopping
___ exercising

___ day dreaming

___ cleaning the house

___ visiting people out of obligation

___ visiting people for fun

___ volunteer work I truly enjoy

___ volunteer work out of obligation

___ a job I truly enjoy

___ job out of necessity

___ quality time with own family

___ baby-sitting I enjoy

___ baby-sitting out of obligation

___ time with own family out of necessity/obligation

___ spiritual activities I truly enjoy

___ spiritual activities out of guilt

___ drinking or getting high

___ going to parties

___ working on the house or garden

___ counseling friends in trouble

___ doing favors for people

___ taking courses

_____

_____

_____

5. **Reflect on how you spend your time.** Take a minute now to evaluate what you do with your time. Do the activities that take up most of your time support your life values? If not, do they actually *detract* from your life values?

6. **Write a mission statement.** Now that you have a good idea of how you actually spend your time compared to how you *want* to spend your time, write a mission statement. What do you have a burning passion to achieve in life? How must you

reorganize your time to support your values? Which activities must you drop, and which must you spend more time on? If one value takes precedence over the others, emphasize that in your statement. Write your statement as if it has already happened. Be specific.

Example:

If your top five values were "excellent physical health, inner peace, financial success, a loving relationship with my significant other, a loving relationship with my children," your mission statement might look something like this:

"Five years from now I am eating right and exercising regularly. I spend an hour each day meditating. I have curtailed relationships with people who drain me emotionally. I have $100,000 invested in mutual funds earning 10 percent profit per year. My spouse and I take time for romance every day and we enjoy each other's company. I also dedicate one day each week to having fun with my children."

Write your mission statement:

_____

_____

_____

_____

_____

_____

EXERCISE 4

Identify Leaders in Your Life

1. List five people you know who have strong Leader characteristics:

_____

_____

_____

_____

_____

2. **Think about an incident you observed when a friend acted like a Leader.** Perhaps she inspired you and others to do something that you feared, or she took charge in a crisis and assumed all responsibility. Write down details about the Leader behaviors your friend exhibited, including how she looked, talked, and acted.

_____

_____

_____

_____

3. **Recall an incident in which your parents or siblings acted like Leaders.** Describe the incident, and record details about how your family member looked, sounded, and acted.

_____

_____

_____

_____

_____

_____

4. **Recall an incident in which your boss or one of your co-workers acted like a Leader.** Again, record details about the incident and about the person's appearance, voice, and actions.

_____

_____

_____

_____

5. **Now go back through each of the incidents you wrote about above, and remember how you felt as you observed your friend, your family member, and your boss or colleague act like a Leader.** Were you frightened? Proud? Intimidated? Inspired? Write down the feelings you remember having during and after each incident. This will give you a clue about your own readiness to become a Leader.

    Incident #1:

_____

_____

_____

Incident #2:

_____

_____

_____

Incident #3:

_____

_____

_____

EXERCISE 5

Reverse a Bad Leadership
Experience from Your Past

1. **Remember a time in the past when you were in a leader-
    ship role and messed up badly.** Perhaps you became auto-
    cratic and got everyone angry at you, or you were too
    frightened to assert your authority and so let things get out
    of control. Describe the incident, including details about how
    you looked, spoke, and acted during and after the incident.

    _____

    _____

    _____

    _____

    _____

_____

2. What should you have done that you failed to do?

    _____

    _____

    _____

    _____

    _____

    _____

3. How would a balanced Leader handle that same situation?

    _____

    _____

    _____

    _____

    _____

4. Reenact the situation, this time acting like a Leader. Warm
    up by reviewing Exercises 1 and 2.

Role-play Exercises

This section contains exercises to help you practice your Leader skills in typical everyday situations. You can practice these alone, but you'll get even better results if you do them with a partner. These exercises will prepare you to act like a Leader in real-life situations.

EXERCISE 6

The Hand-Off Maneuver

The Situation: You just got appointed head of a fund-raising committee, your least favorite activity. To make matters worse, nobody on the committee feels terribly motivated to do the dirty work fund-raising involves.

Your Task: Lead the meeting, ensuring that tasks do get assigned and that you don't end up doing all the work yourself. Try to motivate committee members so that they actually want to do what must be done.

Suggested Episodes to Watch in Preparation:

- ❑ "The Emissary" *(TNG):* Picard assigns Worf to work with his ex-girlfriend, in spite of Worf's strong objections.
- ❑ "Necessary Evil" *(DS9):* Gul Dukat assigns Odo to investigate a crime in spite of Odo's reluctance.

How to Proceed: Prepare an inspiring statement about your goal, and try to motivate people by bringing their attention to that goal. Also prepare a detailed list of the tasks to accomplish. Ask for volunteers, and if nobody steps forward, ask people to assume responsibility. Try to affirm strengths that people bring as you assign them tasks ("You have such great organizational skills, so you'd do a great job in planning the auction").

EXERCISE 7

Rules of Evaluation

The Situation: You are the manager of a five-person department. You recently completed a three-page performance review on one of your subordinates, Jack. You gave Jack top marks in all categories. He is an excellent worker. Your boss saw his performance review and asked you to change some numbers to lower ratings.

Your Task: Go back to your boss and tell him that you believe Jack performed very well and that you want to leave the ratings as they are.

Suggested Episodes to Watch in Preparation:

- ❑ "The Measure of a Man" *(TNG):* Picard challenges Starfleet and goes to bat for Data.
- ❑ "The Offspring" *(TNG):* Picard does it for Data again.
- ❑ "Dax" *(DS9):* Sisko insists that Dax must have a hearing after she gets accused of treason.

How to Proceed: Make sure you know exactly what you're going to say to your boss. Be prepared with facts and whatever data will convince your boss. Remain polite, honest, and quite determined in your conversation with your boss, and prepare to accept the consequences of challenging him.

EXERCISE 8

The Trouble with Quibbles

The Situation: Your church group is planning a special service on Native American religions as part of an interdenominational exchange. You have a strong interest in Native American culture and some expertise in that area. You feel motivated to head the planning committee, although you never stepped forward before in your ten years of church membership. Another person, well known to the group as a good organizer, has also expressed interest in leading the planning committee.

Your Task: Make a case to convince the group to assign leadership to you.

Suggested Episode to Watch in Preparation:

❑ "Redemption, Part II" *(TNG):* Data asks Picard for a shot at a Captain's position.

How to Proceed: Express your interest in the leadership role without hesitation or apology. Tell why you believe you would be the best person for the job, and how you would proceed if you do take charge. Prepare for both outcomes: accepting graciously if assigned the position; accepting rejection gracefully if the other contender gets chosen.

PART SIX

INTERDEPENDENCE

ON THE BRIDGE

16

THE SEVEN CARDINAL

VIRTUES OF HEROES

No one can whistle a symphony. It takes an orchestra to play it.
—Halford E. Luccock

Can you imagine what would happen in the United States if the President suddenly found himself alone in the White House, without staff or advisors? How would h answer his mail, determine a budget, or set health care policy How would he prepare a banquet for visiting dignitaries, c choose which bash to attend?

Most endeavors on earth require teamwork. You can't run corporation without a staff, or a ship without a crew. As belov so above: the *Star Trek* characters survive in space by workin together.

When things look grim on the final frontier, Kirk depends o Scotty to make impossible repairs and on Spock to come up wit a way out of the predicament. The entire crew depends on Kir to give the orders and intuitively choose the right course of action.

In the classic episode "The Doomsday Machine," a giant weapon of war attacks the *Enterprise* after annihilating every planet in its path and severely damaging the spaceship *Constellation*. Kirk decides to man the remains of the *Constellation* and ram it into the killing machine, risking his own life. Meanwhile, Spock takes command of the *Enterprise*, and Scotty manages to keep both ships running, then to beam Kirk out just before the *Constellation* explodes. Fortunately, Kirk's plan works—he saves the cosmos from destruction—but he couldn't have done it without Scotty's help, and *wouldn't* have done it if Spock hadn't been able to take over for him.

This same pattern repeats in episode after episode. The crew works together seamlessly, and so defeats the foe. When Jean-Luc discovers the space anomaly in "All Good Things . . . ," he rallies Data, La Forge, Worf, and Bev Crusher to help him save the day, despite the fact that he has a degenerative brain disease and his plans seem irrational. Worf and Riker manage to work together, though they are at phasers drawn over their mutual love, Deanna. The crew stands together in spite of difficulties, and so they destroy the anomaly and the universe survives.

For a team to function well, it needs a balanced mix of all the heroic types. Although Picard may have stellar character, an entire ship full of Picards would be a space nightmare. You can't have "all chiefs and no Indians." Leaders set the pace and call the shots, but without Relaters to balance them out, life becomes all work and no fun. Similarly, you can't surpass Troi or Guinan for kindness and compassion, but a ship carrying only Relaters would be the joke of the Quadrant. Instead of exploring strange new worlds, the ship would become Esalen in the skies: a space retreat where crewmembers could process their feelings without end while nasty alien beasties took over the universe.

The *Star Trek* crew faces no such dangers. Troi leans on Picard for a sense of direction; Picard has Guinan to keep him balanced; Worf relies on Data and Troi for help keeping his hand off his phaser; and Data has the whole crew to help him act human. In times of trouble, each member of the crew plays his or her part in perfect concert with the others, creating a symphony of harmonious and effective action.

In reality, few teams run as smoothly as on *Star Trek*. "Every great man eventually resents a partner in greatness," said Marcus Annaeus Lucan, the Roman poet. In most collaborations, serious jealousies and resentments eventually get in the way; groups break up, members quit, internal rifts destroy productivity. The Beatles split up when their love lives and creative interests propelled them in different directions. Jeffrey Katzenberg broke away from his boss and fellow Hollywood hit-maker, Michael Eisner, and shook the Disney Empire. Half the marriages in the United States end in divorce. That's why organizational psychologists and family therapists stay so busy and make such big bucks.

So what's the *Star Trek* secret? What lessons can we learn from observing interactions on the Bridge?

1. The crewmembers accept themselves as they are.

All the *Star Trek* characters feel comfortable in their own roles: Worf doesn't long to be Science Officer, Data has no interest in a security job, and Picard doesn't pine to become ship empath. Nobody vies for the Captain's chair; every crewmember recognizes that the Captain suits the position best. Spock says to Kirk in "Mirror, Mirror," "I do not desire the Captain's seat. I much prefer my scientific duties."

How many problems in life result from when people refuse to accept their own strengths and weaknesses? In the corporation, people vie for positions that don't suit them, which they can't handle. Dr. Lawrence J. Peter coined a term for this phenomenon: The Peter Principle. This refers to the way people keep getting promoted until they reach a level beyond their capacity, at which they become incompetent. The Peter Principle applies to situations beyond the corporation: The lawyer wants to be a writer, though he has no writing talent.

The writer, on the other hand, wants to be a lawyer, though she has no eye for detail. The high school kid wants to be a prom queen instead of a math whiz—being prom queen seems infinitely cooler. Meanwhile, the prom queen pines for a quicker brain, discounting her ease with people as irrelevant.

And so it goes. We get jealous of others because we don't have a clue what *we're* good for. If we *do* identify our own talents, we undervalue them. Somebody else's assets always seem more glamorous and important than our own.

The *Star Trek* characters enjoy their own roles because they have taken those roles to the highest evolution, which means that each character manifests not only his or her dominant heroic type, but also a range of subsidiary heroic traits as well. Kirk doesn't envy Spock his Analyst post because he has developed his own inner Analyst as much as he needs to, as illustrated in "Arena," when he realizes that he has the makings of gunpowder and, thus, the means to defeat the Gorn. Troi doesn't crave the Captain's chair because she has access to her own inner Leader, as she proves by taking command of the Bridge in "Disaster." When you develop all your internal heroes and achieve balance within yourself, you don't desire what others possess because you have your own "inner wealth."

2.   They believe in themselves.

The *Star Trek* characters know what their special talents are, and what they stink at. That's what makes the teamwork on the Bridge so impeccable: Each character has enough humility to step aside when someone else can do a better job, yet enough self-confidence to step forward and meet challenges with gusto when it makes sense to do so.

You don't see displays of false modesty on the Bridge. Without a hint of conceit, the crewmembers claim their own accomplishments and abilities. When Picard tells the crew that they are "the finest in Starfleet," nobody blushes; nobody says, "Gosh, not really . . . you're just saying that." When Janeway needs a pilot to fly a dangerous mission, Paris steps forward and declares himself the "best pilot aboard."

How many times in life have you downplayed your own abilities because you didn't want to step on somebody's else's toes, look like a braggart, or risk failing? Can you imagine what would happen if Scotty abdicated his post at a critical moment to some more senior—but less competent—Engineer? Or if he had an insecurity attack in the middle of making repairs, fearing that he would make mistakes? It isn't only Scotty's genius that saves the *Enterprise* time after time; it's also his willingness to stick his neck out and assert his genius.

Our warped sense of decorum—"Don't look bad in front of others"; "Don't steal the limelight"—ends up costing us too many opportunities. *Star Trek* shows us that by boldly claiming our abilities and offering to share them, we have nothing to lose—and a universe to gain.

3. They trust each other implicitly and have tremendous faith in each other's talents.

Imagine how great life would be if everyone recognized your unique genius, and if you never envied anyone else's. Can you conceive of a work environment where every single person on staff appreciated, respected, and understood what you do? Where all of your colleagues supported and encouraged you? One where you got assigned to roles that maximized your talents, where your boss trusted you more than you trust yourself, and where power struggles did not exist because everyone loved his or her own job?

That's life on a *Star Trek* vessel. The trust that the *Star Trek* characters give to each other inspires each one to do better. It's no secret that when people expect you to fail, you probably will. Students who get stuck in "stupid" classes do poorly in school; when they get transferred to an advanced track—or when they

luck out and get a teacher like Jaime Escalante of Los Angeles—
they suddenly and surprisingly excel. If your boss tells you that
you screw everything up, you undoubtedly will; if your boss
says you're the most competent person on the face of the Earth,
your capacity amazingly increases. Like a magnet, we draw forth
from others what we expect from them; when we see their worst,
we invoke it; when we see their best, we bring it to the fore.

In "Parallax," B'Elanna Torres gets recommended for the post
of Chief Engineer. She doubts her own ability to fill the position
because she didn't graduate from Starfleet Academy and has
trouble getting along with colleagues (she recently punched a fellow crewman in the nose). But B'Elanna's problems don't deter
Captain Janeway, who has great faith in her and convinces her
that she can do the job. Janeway promotes B'Elanna over the person in line for the post—who happens to be the same guy
B'Elanna cuffed. When B'Elanna later encounters him in the
engine room, he congratulates her and treats her with genuine
deference, clearly recognizing her superior abilities. Each
crewmember acknowledges—and admires—exceptional gifts in
the others.

In contrast, what happens in the corporate world if some
upstart underling gets promoted? Bloodshed! People resign in a
huff, try to sabotage the new boss, gossip wickedly. And in the
end, productivity goes down and good workers quit or get fired
for having a bad attitude.

The *Star Trek* crew can't afford such trouble. If jealousy reigns
on the Bridge and people fight for power, they certainly won't
survive many missions. Can you imagine facing a Romulan war-
ship while fighting over who gets to fire the phasers?

It seems that our *Star Trek* heroes find greater reward in mining
each others' strengths than they do in asserting their own superiority. Why? Because they get back even more than they give.
When someone recognizes your talent and encourages you, you
want to help them in turn. Picard acknowledges Worf's valor,
and in so doing increases it; Worf in turn acknowledges

LaForge's technical competence, increasing it; LaForge admires Data's genius, and Data reveres Picard's leadership, completing the circle. By encouraging each other, the crew creates a self-perpetuating system of reinforcement, always drawing out the best in each other. That tactic works in real life, too. When people recognize your talent and encourage you, you want to help them in turn.

4. They trust the Captain's judgment implicitly.

If your boss snapped out orders at you faster than phaser fire—without saying "please"—would you happily do as told, mouth closed? The *Star Trek* crewmembers do. Watch any episode from any series, and you'll see the Captain bossing everyone around nonstop. Aboard Starfleet vessels, Captains don't bother with the "magic word." They don't need to: The crew does what the Captain orders, no questions asked, no offense taken.

That's because they revere the Captain. In episode after episode, Kirk, Picard, Sisko, and Janeway prove to be the cleverest beings in the galaxy; and their crewmembers have taken note. They believe wholeheartedly in their captains' integrity and competence. If the Captain says "raise shields" when an enemy ship appears, nobody balks. If she declares "red alert" when everything seems hunky dory, that's fine, too. When Picard seemingly loses his marbles in "All Good Things . . . " and goes on a death mission, he still rallies Data, La Forge, Crusher, and Worf to help, because they have so much faith in him.

Can you imagine giving your boss such unconditional obedience? Doubtful. And why should you? Many bosses on Earth rise to power only through ambition, connections, or sheer longevity. The Peter Principal often rules life on Earth, but not life in space. To become a Starfleet Captain, you have to be smarter, craftier, quicker, and more impeccable than everyone else. If *your* boss had Picard's attributes, you just might enjoy doing as told.

One other thing about Starfleet Captains: They treat their subordinates with unshakable respect and kindness. They elicit loyalty because they give and give to the crew. The crew knows the Captain will do anything for them; in turn, they'll do anything for their chief.

5. They enjoy being part of a great team more than being great individually.

When the game is on the line, all the top players ask for the ball. Michael Jordan of the Chicago Bulls publicly declared that the team was his supporting cast. The Police broke up so that Sting could perform on his own; Rob Morrow left the *Northern Exposure* ensemble in the cold, so he could go after more glamorous roles. Human nature drives us to set ourselves apart, to be greater than our cohorts, and more lovable and more beautiful and smarter, too.

Not so for our Starfleet heroes. To serve aboard the *Enterprise*—to reap the friendship and support of the greatest crew in space—is the paramount goal. Riker refuses three promotions to captain his own ship because he'd rather remain part of the *Enterprise* crew. Picard nixes a chance to become commandant of Starfleet Academy to stay on the *Enterprise* in "Coming of Age." Kirk gets restless in his role as Admiral, and jumps at the chance to pilot his beloved ship again in *Star Trek: The Motion Picture*.

What drives the *Star Trek* characters to favor life with the group even over individual eminence? If you've ever had a burst of patriotism or team spirit, you know how it stirs your soul to feel part of something greater than yourself—whether part of a great corporation, a great country, or an unbeatable Little League team. It's the sense that, by joining with others, you become more than what you were before.

In real life, though, that thrill doesn't usually last. So how does the *Star Trek* crew manage to happily hang together over time, avoiding the disillusionment that besets most collaborations?

For one thing, the characters have enough clarity to recognize their need for each other: Kirk the Leader definitely needs Spock the Analyst to help him make the right decisions. Kira the Warrior desperately needs Sisko the Leader to keep her aggression in check. Data the Analyst needs Relaters to teach him about emotion. And can you imagine how lonely a Leader like Kirk, Picard, or Sisko might get with no Relater nearby?

Also, the crewmembers keep their egos stashed in the cargo bay. By the twenty-third century, sentient beings seem to conquer the need to outdo each other, and instead, reap the benefits of mutual support and admiration. Who wouldn't want to give up lonely personal glory for all that excitement, encouragement, and cozy love on the Bridge?

6. They forgive each other's mistakes.

In "Coming of Age," Wesley flunks his Starfleet exams and goes into a tailspin. "I failed you and I failed the *Enterprise*," he wails to Picard. Instead of grounding him, though, Picard urges him to keep his chin up: "Ridiculous! Did you do your best? . . . Wesley, you have to measure your successes and failures within." Similarly, in *Deep Space Nine*, Sisko looks the other way when O'Brien violates every Starfleet regulation to help the prisoner Tosk escape. And when love blinds McCoy to the real nature of his old girlfriend Nancy (now possessed by a murderous alien), his cohorts forgive him even after he nearly leads them to their death.

Aboard the *Enterprise*, the past is space dust. So what if Picard had deadly intent during his Borg escapade? Nobody holds it against him, because he couldn't help it: The Borg made him do it. Even Sisko forgives him, though Picard-as-Borg led the attack that killed Sisko's wife.

How many grudges do you still hold against people who acted like the Borg? Did you ever consider that maybe you should forgive them because unseen powers control their moods and behaviors as totally as the Borg controlled Picard? People get sick, they get hormone overload, they have money problems, in-law problems, too much pressure, problems with Mom and Dad. These things make all humans act nutty, though we hope that people remember us for our better days.

Ten light-years from home, people realize how much they need their pals, and don't worry so much about how this one said something offensive and that one never delivered on a promise. In the vastness of the Final Frontier, the wrongs of fellow mortals seem to find their proper perspective.

7. They play together, mourn together, and go to each other for help.

"Familiarity breeds contempt," goes the old adage. "Don't work with your spouse, date colleagues, or spend too much time with any one person." "Absence makes the heart grow fonder."

Aboard a *Star Trek* vessel, such Earthly wisdom has no gravity. If Picard gets sick of Crusher, he can't move to another city. All he can do is withdraw to his ready room. Living and working in close proximity to the same old characters doesn't seem to grate on our *Star Trek* heroes, though. Instead, they develop real intimacy and rely heavily on each other.

Like old school chums, the crew goes through everything together. They jointly face the death of their friends, like when Tasha Yar dies in the *Next Generation* episode "Skin of Evil." They face their own mortality in crisis after crisis. They become vulnerable together, like when the entire crew gets bombed by mood-altering spores in "This Side of Paradise," or when Kirk and Spock both break down emotionally in "The Naked Time." They even hang out together—the *Deep Space Nine* bunch lets down at Quark's bar; the *Next Gen* folks have fun in the holodeck; and the *Voyager* crew shoots pool.

Why don't the *Star Trek* characters get sick of each other? Maybe because they all have ample self-confidence. In life, when people lack self-esteem, they become tiresome. Insecurity makes once-fun people lash out because they feel inferior. They compete with you; cling to you like chewing gum; lie and put on airs. The *Star Trek* characters don't degenerate into such pettiness or clinginess because they enjoy being themselves, and so they remain eternally enjoyable to be around.

The *Star Trek* characters *do* have their dark moments, but unlike most mortals, they don't hide out and brood when the going gets rough. Instead, they quickly seek help, feeling no shame in asking friends or colleagues for guidance. When Data can't figure out how to love Jenna, he interviews the entire crew looking for clues. When Troi loses her empathic abilities, she takes counsel from her friends. All the captains ask their subordinates for advice in crisis situations. Most of us try to "tough out" the rough times, but Starfleet allows no such silliness. All Starships get assigned a Counselor, and the crew flocks for advice. In fact, Janeway bemoans the lack of a ship's counselor on *Voyager*, and so tries to contact her "animal guide" instead. Because the crew processes problems as they arise, nothing seethes under the surface, no old wounds cause friction over time. Communication stays open and honest and the crewmembers stay friends.

※

Almost every *Star Trek* episode shows exemplary teamwork saving the day. Together, the crew faces danger, each member plays his or her part without hesitation, and together they accomplish what none could do alone. The crew is synergistic: The whole is definitely greater, more indomitable, than the sum of its parts. Certainly, Picard stands above most mortals, but alone, without Data and Worf by his side, he could say "engage" from now until eternity but he wouldn't get even one light-year from home. And where would Data the Great be without Picard, without LaForge? Disassembled, no doubt.

Western culture glorifies individuality. "Being all that you can be" means going it alone, crushing the competition. Scientists at Johns Hopkins compete with researchers at Harvard to find a cure for AIDS. Politicians fight over whose gun-control legislation to accept, debating for years, while kids shoot each other on the streets. The United States races with the Soviet Union to get the first man on the moon. You compete with your neighbor to grow the biggest tomatoes.

What if you did the *Star Trek* thing and joined forces with your neighbor? You might actually grow bigger tomatoes. In fact, if all the great tomato growers in your town got together and pooled ideas, you might well develop monster Beefsteaks and all become rich. In the same way, if all the greatest scientists in the world openly shared their research, they could accomplish so much more, so much sooner. But sadly, few scientists want to share a Nobel Prize. It takes a true hero to share selflessly with others, to forgo personal glory for the joy of giving to a group. So how does all this beautiful philosophy about teamwork apply to your life? You probably don't have a Starfleet-caliber team in place. It isn't likely that a fearsome Warrior will suddenly appear at your desk when your boss next insults you, or that a Leader will show up at your doorstep tonight, telling you what to do with your floundering life.

The reality is, you're on your own for now. There's a saying in Eastern philosophy: "When the student is ready, the teacher appears." In the same way, if you want to find a group of like-minded and inspiring people to build a lasting collaboration with, you need to get ready. First, *you* must become a worthy team member yourself.

How? By applying the lessons for creating a team in your own psyche. All the various heroes within *you* must come forward and work together in harmony, so that you aren't always looking to the outside world to save you. Instead of waiting for a Warrior to rescue you when your boss goes off the deep end, you need to call forth your own inner Warrior and stand up for yourself. At the same time, you need to call forth your Analyst so you don't go overboard and commit murder. Likewise, you can't count on a Relater-figure to supply the love in your life: You need to find the love within yourself, or you'll be eternally dependent on somebody else. Until you have inner poise, you'll make a lousy, needy partner and team member.

So start with Virtue #1: Accept yourself as you are, even if you don't make conversation as easily as your Relater peers, and you can't make decisions as readily as your Leader colleagues. You need to identify your own strengths and then cherish them. Then take the other steps for building teamwork—believe in yourself, trust yourself, and know that you have a wealth of heroic qualities you can call on when the need arises.

Let your Warrior stand up for what is true and right.

Let your Analyst guide your mind.

Let your Relater guide your heart.

Let your Leader come forward to reveal your mission and inspire you to fulfill it.

Once you call forth your own inner heroes, you can engage in the final heroic act: joining with others to boldly transform the world into a more peaceful, compassionate place. The Earth desperately needs Starfleet-ready members—people of impeccable courage and integrity, and it desperately needs these highly evolved individuals to join together to establish a more peaceful, progressive, loving universe.

And so, the message of this book is this: Don't sit around waiting for a better day to dawn. Boldly live your life, starting now. Summon your inner heroes, become the hero you were destined to become—and then find a good crew to aim for the stars with. Together, we *can* make it so.

A NOTE FROM THE AUTHORS

We hope you enjoyed reading this book, and we'd love to hear how the exercises worked for you. Please let us know. You can write to us at:

BOLDLY LIVE
P.O. Box 471
Littleton, MA 01460

In addition, we offer video tapes, audio cassettes, workbooks, seminars, and retreats in personal growth and development for individuals and organizations. Learn to fully express your LEADER, WARRIOR, ANALYST, and RELATER moment-by-moment, by bringing out the heroic style that will most effectively help you to achieve your personal and organizational goals. For more information, contact:

Richard Raben
P.O. Box 3392
Framingham, MA 01701
(800) 555-9598